2023 UK
Air Fryer
Cookbook

Healthy and Fast & Fresh Air Fryer Recipes for Your
Whole Family to Fry, Bake, Grill, and Roast (European
Measurements & UK Ingredients)

Sean K. Rupert

Contents

Chapter 4 Fish and Seafood 33

Chapter 5 Beef, Pork, and Lamb 44

Chapter 6 Vegetables and Sides 56

Introduction

As a seasoned chef, I've always been a bit skeptical of air fryers. I mean, how could something that doesn't involve hot oil produce the same results as deep-frying? But then, I decided to give them a chance and found that there's more to these gadgets than meets the eye.In this recipe book, I aim to provide a comprehensive guide on air frying, covering its definition, functionality, and advantages. Additionally, I will share my personal collection of top air fryer recipes, accompanied by useful tips and techniques to help you maximize your air frying experience.

For home cooks, air fryers are a game-changer. They are incredibly easy to use and require very little clean-up. They cook food quickly and evenly, which is great for things like frozen appetisers or chicken wings. Plus, they use less oil than traditional frying methods, which means that the food is healthier and less greasy. I was blown away by how versatile and convenient air fryers were. My advice to anyone who wants to try out air fryers is to experiment and have fun with it.You can make all kinds of creative dishes that are healthy and delicious, all without sacrificing the taste and texture that you love. So, don't be afraid to give air fryers a try – who knows, you might just discover a new favourite way to cook!

I constantly experimented with new recipes and ideas, and before I knew it, I had a collection of fantastic air fryer recipes. That's when it hit me: I needed to share my passion and knowledge with others. Writing a cookbook seemed like the perfect way to showcase just how amazing air-fried foods can be. So, I set out to create a comprehensive guide, filled with delicious and creative recipes that anyone could make. It was a labour of love, and I couldn't be more thrilled with the result!

As the chef and author of this air fryer cookbook, I am thrilled to introduce you to the world of air frying. Cooking is my passion, and I love experimenting with new techniques and ingredients to create amazing dishes. That's why I have poured my heart and soul into this cookbook, testing and refining every recipe to ensure that you get the best possible results. From classic appetisers to exotic main courses, from crunchy snacks to delectable desserts, my recipes showcase just how versatile and tasty air-fried foods can be. But that's not all! I have also included plenty of tips and tricks to help you get the most out of your air fryer. Whether you're a beginner or an experienced air fryer user, these tips will help you take your cooking to the next level.

As you try out these recipes, I would love to hear from you about your experiences and feedback. Grab your air fryer, fire it up, and let's get cooking!

What Are Air Fryers?

Air fryers are an exciting kitchen appliance that have taken the world by storm in recent years. The way air fryers work is simple yet ingenious. They use a powerful heating element to heat up the air inside the fryer, which is then circulated around the food using a high-speed fan. This creates a crispy, crunchy exterior while keeping the inside moist and tender. Some air fryers even have multiple cooking racks, allowing you to cook multiple items at once.

For beginners:

Air fryers are an excellent addition to any kitchen, especially for those who are new to cooking. They can help you create delicious, crispy food with minimal effort. All you need to do is place your food in the fryer basket, set the temperature and time according to the recipe, and let the fryer do the rest. Air fryers are also a healthier alternative to deep frying, as they require little or no oil to cook your food. Plus, air fryers are compact and easy to store, making them a great choice for smaller kitchens.

For experienced cooks:

If you're an experienced cook looking for a new kitchen gadget to add to your collection, an air fryer might be just what you need. And because air fryers require little or no oil, you can experiment with different flavour combinations without worrying about adding extra fat and calories. Additionally, air fryers are often faster than traditional oven cooking, making them a convenient option for busy households. So if you're looking for a new way to cook up some tasty treats, consider giving an air fryer a try.

How to choose an air fryer?

Are you ready to take your cooking to the next level with an air fryer? Choosing the right air fryer can seem like a daunting task with so many options available on the market. But fear not, I am here to guide you through the process step by step! By following these guidelines, you can choose an air fryer that will suit your needs and preferences.

Step 1: Determine your budget

The first step is to determine how much you are willing to spend on an air fryer. The price of air fryers can range from less than $50 to over $300, so it's important to set a budget and stick to it.

Step 2: Consider the size

Air fryers come in a variety of sizes, so it's important to choose one that will meet your cooking needs. If you're cooking for one or two people, a smaller air fryer may suffice, while larger families may need a bigger model. Consider the capacity of the fryer, which is measured in quarts, to determine whether it will be big enough for your needs.

Step 3: Look for features

Consider the features that you need in an air fryer, such as temperature control, a timer, and pre-set cooking programs. Some air fryers come with additional accessories like baking pans and racks, which can add value and versatility to your cooking.

Step 4: Check the reviews

Read reviews from other customers to get an idea of how well the air fryer performs. Look for feedback on ease of use, cooking performance, and durability.

Step 5: Brand reputation

Consider the brand reputation and warranty when making your decision. Choose a brand that has a good reputation for quality and reliability and offers a warranty that will protect your investment.

What Can You Cook in an Air Fryer and Foods to avoid?

Are you ready to start cooking with your air fryer, but not sure what foods to cook or avoid? Don't worry, I've got you covered! Here are some selection criteria to consider when deciding what to cook and what not to cook in your air fryer.

First, consider the moisture content of the food. Foods with high moisture content, such as fresh fruits and vegetables, may not cook properly in an air fryer. These foods may end up too soft or too dry. On the other hand, foods with a low moisture content, such as meats, fish, and some vegetables like potatoes, are ideal for air frying as they will cook to crispy perfection.

Next, consider the fat content of the food. Foods with high fat content, such as bacon, may not be suitable for air frying as the excess fat can cause smoking and splattering. However, foods with a moderate amount of healthy fat, such as salmon and avocado, are great options for air frying.

When it comes to coatings, be mindful of the type of coating used. Batters and bread crumbs may not cook evenly in an air fryer, leading to unevenly cooked food. However, a light coating of breadcrumbs or a dry rub can add texture and flavour to your air-fried dishes.

Lastly, consider the size and shape of the food. Foods that are too large or oddly shaped may not fit in the air fryer basket or cook evenly. It's best to choose foods that are small enough to fit in the basket and can be arranged in a single layer for even cooking.

The Benefits Of Air Fryers

Looking for a way to enjoy your favourite fried foods without the guilt? Want to save time in the kitchen and cook up delicious meals in minutes? Then an air fryer is the perfect kitchen gadget for you!

1. Healthier cooking: Air frying uses hot air to cook food, eliminating the need for oil or minimal use of oil, making it a healthier alternative to deep-frying. This means that you can enjoy crispy and delicious food without the added calories and unhealthy fats.

2. Time-saving: Air fryers cook food faster than traditional ovens or stovetops. This is because the hot air circulates around the food, cooking it evenly and quickly. You can save time in the kitchen by using an air fryer for quick and easy meals, especially on busy weeknights.

3. Versatility: Air fryers are versatile kitchen appliances that can cook a wide range of foods, from chicken wings and French fries to roasted vegetables and even cakes. You can use an air fryer to grill, bake, roast, or fry your favourite foods.

4. Easy to use: Air fryers are simple and easy to use. All you need to do is preheat the machine, add your food to the basket, and set the temperature and time. You can also find air fryers with pre-set cooking functions that take the guesswork out of cooking.

5. Easy to clean: Most air fryers have non-stick baskets or trays that are easy to clean, making cleanup a breeze. Some models also have dishwasher-safe parts for even easier cleaning.

If any of the following describes you, then you need an air fryer in your life! An air fryer is a perfect addition to any kitchen, offering a healthier, faster, and more convenient way to cook your favourite meals.

1. If you're someone who loves fried foods but wants to cut down on unhealthy fats and calories, an air fryer is the perfect solution. You can indulge in your favourite fried dishes without any of the guilt, and with a wide range of recipes available, you'll never run out of delicious options.

2. For those with busy lifestyles, an air fryer is a game-changer. It saves you time in the kitchen, allowing you to cook up a quick and easy meal in minutes without compromising on taste or quality. You can enjoy a healthy and delicious meal in no time, leaving you with more time to relax and unwind.

3. If you're short on space in your kitchen, an air fryer is an excellent option. It takes up minimal space and is a multi-functional appliance that can replace several kitchen gadgets. This means you can free up valuable counter space while still enjoying all the benefits of a fully-equipped kitchen.

So why wait? Choose an air fryer today and start enjoying healthier, faster, and more delicious meals in the comfort of your own home. Whether you're a health-conscious cook, a busy professional, or a small-space dweller, an air fryer is a must-have kitchen gadget that will make your life easier and more enjoyable.

How to Clean & Maintenance?

Keeping your air fryer clean and well-maintained is crucial for ensuring its performance and longevity. Here are some simple steps you can follow to keep it clean:

1. Unplug the air fryer and let it cool down before cleaning.
2. Remove the basket and tray from the air fryer and soak them in warm soapy water for 10-15 minutes.
3. Use a non-abrasive sponge or cloth to wipe the inside of the air fryer, removing any food particles or grease. You can also use a toothbrush or q-tip to clean hard-to-reach areas.
4. Rinse the basket and tray thoroughly and dry them with a clean towel or let them air dry.
5. Wipe down the outside of the air fryer with a damp cloth, being careful not to get water inside the appliance.
6. Reassemble the air fryer and store it in a dry place.

To maintain your air fryer, you should also follow these additional steps:

1. Check the manual for specific maintenance instructions and tips.
2. Use only non-abrasive sponges and cleaning solutions to avoid scratching the surface.
3. Avoid using metal utensils or abrasive cleaners that can damage the non-stick coating.
4. Regularly check and clean the air intake vents to prevent clogs and ensure proper air circulation.
5. Replace any damaged parts or accessories as needed.

The frequency of cleaning and maintenance depends on how often you use your air fryer. If you use it daily or multiple times a week, it's recommended to clean it after every use. If you use it less frequently, you can clean it once a week or every few uses.

The care tips with Air Fryers

Great to hear that you're interested in taking care of your air fryer, which is essential to make sure it lasts a long time and stays in good condition! Here are some care tips to help you keep your appliance working like new! By following these tips, your air fryer can be ensured to stay in tip-top shape and continues to provide you with healthy meals for years to come.

First things first, make sure you read the instruction manual before using your air fryer. This gives you important information about how to properly use and care for your appliance.

When it comes to cleaning, it's best to clean your air fryer after every use. I already talked about this earlier, so I'll just say it again real quick. Remove the fryer basket and accessories, and wash them in warm, soapy water. Wipe down the inside of the fryer with a damp cloth to remove any leftover food debris.

For a deeper clean, take apart the appliance and clean all the individual parts every few weeks. Check the instruction manual for specific details on how to do this. It's important to use the right cooking spray to avoid damaging the non-stick coating of the fryer basket. Be sure to use a cooking spray that is specifically designed for air fryers. Avoid using harsh cleaners or abrasive materials, as they can also damage the non-stick coating. Stick to gentle cleaning solutions like warm, soapy water. And lastly, store your air fryer in a cool dry place away from direct sunlight and humid environments. Because high temperatures and humidity can cause the non-stick coating inside the air fryer to degrade, which can affect the quality of the food you cook in it.

Frequently Asked Questions

Q: Can you use an air fryer to cook frozen foods?

A: Yes, you can cook frozen foods in an air fryer. In fact, many frozen foods such as french fries, chicken tenders, and fish fillets are perfect for air frying. Just be sure to adjust the cooking time and temperature according to the instructions on the packaging.

Q: How much food can you cook in an air fryer at once?

A: The amount of food you can cook in an air fryer at once depends on the size of the air fryer. Typically, a standard-size air fryer can hold 1-2 servings of food, while a larger air fryer can hold up to 4 servings.

Q: Can I cook multiple items at once in my air fryer?

A: Yes, you can cook multiple items at once in your air fryer as long as there is enough space for the air to circulate around each item. If you're cooking items with different cooking times or temperatures, you may need to adjust the cooking time or remove the items at different times.

Q: Can you use an air fryer to bake?

A: Yes, you can use an air fryer to bake, and it's a great way to make small batches of baked goods like cookies, brownies, and cakes. Just be sure to use the appropriate baking accessories and adjust the cooking time and temperature accordingly.

Q: Can I put aluminium foil or parchment paper in my air fryer?

A: Yes, you can use aluminium foil or parchment paper in your air fryer, but you need to make sure that it is properly placed and does not cover the entire basket. If the foil or paper covers the entire basket, it can restrict airflow and affect the cooking process. It is also important to make sure that the foil or paper does not come into contact with the heating element, as this can cause a fire hazard. Additionally, be sure to use high-quality, non-toxic foil or paper that is safe for cooking.

Q: How long does it take to cook food in an air fryer?

A: The cooking time in an air fryer depends on the type and amount of food you are cooking. Generally, most foods take between 10-20 minutes to cook in an air fryer. However, it's important to check the food frequently and adjust the cooking time as needed.

Q: Is it safe to leave my air fryer unattended while it's in use?

A: It's generally safe to leave your air fryer unattended while it's in use, but it's always best to be cautious and check on it periodically. Make sure that the air fryer is placed on a stable surface away from any flammable materials and that the cord is not in a position where it could be tripped over.

Q: How do I know when my food is done cooking in the air fryer?

A: Most air fryers come with a timer and temperature control that you can use to set the cooking time and temperature. Once the timer goes off, check your food for doneness by using a meat thermometer or by cutting into it to make sure it's cooked all the way through. If it's not done yet, you can always put it back in the air fryer for a few more minutes.

Chapter 1 Breakfasts

Not-So-English Muffins

Serves 4

Prep time: 5 minutes / Cook time: 10 minutes

Ingredients:

- 2 strips turkey bacon, cut in half crosswise
- 2 whole-grain English muffins, split
- 235 ml fresh baby spinach, long stems removed
- ¼ ripe pear, peeled and thinly sliced
- 4 slices low-moisture Mozzarella or other melting cheese

Instructions:

1. Place bacon strips in air fryer basket and air fry at 200ºC for 2 minutes. Check and separate strips if necessary so they cook evenly. Cook for 3 to 4 more minutes, until crispy. Remove and drain on paper towels.
2. Place split muffin halves in air fryer basket and cook for 2 minutes, just until lightly browned.
3. Open air fryer and top each muffin with a quarter of the baby spinach, several pear slices, a strip of bacon, and a slice of cheese.
4. Air fry at 182ºC for 1 to 2 minutes, until cheese completely melts.

Greek Bagels

Makes 2 bagels

Prep time: 10 minutes / Cook time: 10 minutes

Ingredients:

- 120 ml self-raising flour, plus more for dusting
- 120 ml plain Greek yoghurt
- 1 egg
- 1 tablespoon water
- 4 teaspoons sesame seeds or za'atar
- Cooking oil spray
- 1 tablespoon butter, melted

Instructions:

1. In a large bowl, using a wooden spoon, stir together the flour and yoghurt until a tacky dough forms. Transfer the dough to a lightly floured work surface and roll the dough into a ball.
2. Cut the dough into 2 pieces and roll each piece into a log. Form each log into a bagel shape, pinching the ends together.
3. In a small bowl, whisk the egg and water. Brush the egg wash on the bagels.
4. Sprinkle 2 teaspoons of the toppings on each bagel and gently press it into the dough.
5. Insert the crisper plate into the basket and the basket into the unit. Preheat the unit by selecting BAKE, setting the temperature to 166ºC, and setting the time to 3 minutes. Select START/STOP to begin.
6. Once the unit is preheated, spray the crisper plate with cooking spray. Drizzle the bagels with the butter and place them into the basket.
7. Select BAKE, set the temperature to 166ºC, and set the time to 10 minutes. Select START/STOP to begin.
8. When the cooking is complete, the bagels should be lightly golden on the outside. Serve warm.

Apple Cider Doughnut Holes

Makes 10 mini doughnuts

Prep time: 10 minutes / Cook time: 6 minutes

Ingredients:

- Doughnut Holes:
- 350 ml plain flour
- 2 tablespoons granulated sugar
- 2 teaspoons baking powder
- 1 teaspoon baking soda
- ½ teaspoon coarse or flaky salt

- Pinch of freshly grated nutmeg
- 60 ml plus 2 tablespoons buttermilk, chilled
- 2 tablespoons apple cider or apple juice, chilled
- 1 large egg, lightly beaten
- Vegetable oil, for brushing
- Glaze:
- 120 ml icing sugar
- 2 tablespoons unsweetened applesauce
- ¼ teaspoon vanilla extract
- Pinch of coarse or flaky salt

Instructions:

1. Make the doughnut holes: In a bowl, whisk together the flour, granulated sugar, baking powder, baking soda, salt, and nutmeg until smooth. Add the buttermilk, cider, and egg and stir with a small rubber spatula or spoon until the dough just comes together.
2. Using a 28 g ice cream scoop or 2 tablespoons, scoop and drop 10 balls of dough into the air fryer basket, spaced evenly apart, and brush the tops lightly with oil. Air fry at 176°C until the doughnut holes are golden brown and fluffy, about 6 minutes. Transfer the doughnut holes to a wire rack to cool completely.
3. Make the glaze: In a small bowl, stir together the powdered sugar, applesauce, vanilla, and salt until smooth.
4. Dip the tops of the doughnuts holes in the glaze, then let stand until the glaze sets before serving. If you're impatient and want warm doughnuts, have the glaze ready to go while the doughnuts cook, then use the glaze as a dipping sauce for the warm doughnuts, fresh out of the air fryer.

Bacon-and-Eggs Avocado

Serves 1
Prep time: 5 minutes / Cook time: 17 minutes

Ingredients:

- 1 large egg

- 1 avocado, halved, peeled, and pitted
- 2 slices bacon
- Fresh parsley, for serving (optional)
- Sea salt flakes, for garnish (optional)

Instructions:

1. Spray the air fryer basket with avocado oil. Preheat the air fryer to 160°C. Fill a small bowl with cool water.
2. Soft-boil the egg: Place the egg in the air fryer basket. Air fry for 6 minutes for a soft yolk or 7 minutes for a cooked yolk. Transfer the egg to the bowl of cool water and let sit for 2 minutes. Peel and set aside.
3. Use a spoon to carve out extra space in the center of the avocado halves until the cavities are big enough to fit the soft-boiled egg. Place the soft-boiled egg in the center of one half of the avocado and replace the other half of the avocado on top, so the avocado appears whole on the outside.
4. Starting at one end of the avocado, wrap the bacon around the avocado to completely cover it. Use toothpicks to hold the bacon in place.
5. Place the bacon-wrapped avocado in the air fryer basket and air fry for 5 minutes. Flip the avocado over and air fry for another 5 minutes, or until the bacon is cooked to your liking. Serve on a bed of fresh parsley, if desired, and sprinkle with salt flakes, if desired.
6. Best served fresh. Store extras in an airtight container in the fridge for up to 4 days. Reheat in a preheated 160°C air fryer for 4 minutes, or until heated through.

Bacon, Egg, and Cheese Roll Ups

Serves 4
Prep time: 15 minutes / Cook time: 15 minutes

Ingredients:

- 2 tablespoons unsalted butter

- 60 ml chopped onion
- ½ medium green pepper, seeded and chopped
- 6 large eggs
- 12 slices bacon
- 235 ml shredded sharp Cheddar cheese
- 120 ml mild salsa, for dipping

Instructions:

1. In a medium skillet over medium heat, melt butter. Add onion and pepper to the skillet and sauté until fragrant and onions are translucent, about 3 minutes.
2. Whisk eggs in a small bowl and pour into skillet. Scramble eggs with onions and peppers until fluffy and fully cooked, about 5 minutes. Remove from heat and set aside.
3. On work surface, place three slices of bacon side by side, overlapping about ¼ inch. Place 60 ml scrambled eggs in a heap on the side closest to you and sprinkle 60 ml cheese on top of the eggs.
4. Tightly roll the bacon around the eggs and secure the seam with a toothpick if necessary. Place each roll into the air fryer basket.
5. Adjust the temperature to 176ºC and air fry for 15 minutes. Rotate the rolls halfway through the cooking time.
6. Bacon will be brown and crispy when completely cooked. Serve immediately with salsa for dipping.

Hearty Blueberry Oatmeal

Serves 6
Prep time: 10 minutes / Cook time: 25 minutes

Ingredients:

- 350 ml quick oats
- 1¼ teaspoons ground cinnamon, divided
- ½ teaspoon baking powder
- Pinch salt
- 235 ml unsweetened vanilla almond milk
- 60 ml honey

- 1 teaspoon vanilla extract
- 1 egg, beaten
- 475 ml blueberries
- Olive oil
- 1½ teaspoons sugar, divided
- 6 tablespoons low-fat whipped topping (optional)

Instructions:

1. In a large bowl, mix together the oats, 1 teaspoon of cinnamon, baking powder, and salt.
2. In a medium bowl, whisk together the almond milk, honey, vanilla and egg.
3. Pour the liquid ingredients into the oats mixture and stir to combine. Fold in the blueberries.
4. Lightly spray a baking pan with oil.
5. Add half the blueberry mixture to the pan.
6. Sprinkle ⅛ teaspoon of cinnamon and ½ teaspoon sugar over the top.
7. Cover the pan with aluminum foil and place gently in the air fryer basket.
8. Air fry at 182ºC for 20 minutes. Remove the foil and air fry for an additional 5 minutes. Transfer the mixture to a shallow bowl.
9. Repeat with the remaining blueberry mixture, ½ teaspoon of sugar, and ⅛ teaspoon of cinnamon.
10. To serve, spoon into bowls and top with whipped topping.

BLT Breakfast Wrap

Serves 4

Prep time: 5 minutes / Cook time: 10 minutes

Ingredients:

- 230 g reduced-salt bacon
- 8 tablespoons mayonnaise
- 8 large romaine lettuce leaves
- 4 plum tomatoes, sliced
- Salt and freshly ground black pepper, to taste

Instructions:

1. Arrange the bacon in a single layer in the air

fryer basket. (It's OK if the bacon sits a bit on the sides.) Set the air fryer to 176ºC and air fry for 10 minutes. Check for crispiness and air fry for 2 to 3 minutes longer if needed. Cook in batches, if necessary, and drain the grease in between batches.

2. Spread 1 tablespoon of mayonnaise on each of the lettuce leaves and top with the tomatoes and cooked bacon. Season to taste with salt and freshly ground black pepper. Roll the lettuce leaves as you would a burrito, securing with a toothpick if desired.

Bacon Eggs on the Go

Serves 1

Prep time: 5 minutes / Cook time: 15 minutes

Ingredients:

- 2 eggs
- 110 g bacon, cooked
- Salt and ground black pepper, to taste

Instructions:

1. Preheat the air fryer to 204ºC. Put liners in a regular cupcake tin.
2. Crack an egg into each of the cups and add the bacon. Season with some pepper and salt.
3. Bake in the preheated air fryer for 15 minutes, or until the eggs are set. Serve warm.

Homemade Cherry Breakfast Tarts

Serves 6

Prep time: 15 minutes / Cook time: 20 minutes

Ingredients:

Tarts:

- 2 refrigerated piecrusts
- 80 ml cherry preserves
- 1 teaspoon cornflour
- Cooking oil

Frosting:

- 120 ml vanilla yoghurt

- 30 g cream cheese
- 1 teaspoon stevia
- Rainbow sprinkles

Make the Tarts Instructions:

1. Place the piecrusts on a flat surface. Using a knife or pizza cutter, cut each piecrust into 3 rectangles, for 6 total. (I discard the unused dough left from slicing the edges.)
2. In a small bowl, combine the preserves and cornflour. Mix well.
3. Scoop 1 tablespoon of the preserves mixture onto the top half of each piece of piecrust.
4. Fold the bottom of each piece up to close the tart. Using the back of a fork, press along the edges of each tart to seal.
5. Spray the breakfast tarts with cooking oil and place them in the air fryer. I do not recommend stacking the breakfast tarts. They will stick together if stacked. You may need to prepare them in two batches. Bake at 375ºF for 10 minutes.
6. Allow the breakfast tarts to cool fully before removing from the air fryer.
7. If necessary, repeat steps 5 and 6 for the remaining breakfast tarts. Make the Frosting
8. In a small bowl, combine the yoghurt, cream cheese, and stevia. Mix well.
9. Spread the breakfast tarts with frosting and top with sprinkles, and serve.

Apple Rolls

Makes 12 rolls

Prep time: 20 minutes / Cook time: 20 to 24 minutes

Ingredients:

Apple Rolls:

- 475 ml plain flour, plus more for dusting
- 2 tablespoons granulated sugar
- 1 teaspoon salt
- 3 tablespoons butter, at room temperature
- 180 ml milk, whole or semi-skimmed

- 120 ml packed light brown sugar
- 1 teaspoon ground cinnamon
- 1 large Granny Smith apple, peeled and diced
- 1 to 2 tablespoons oil

Icing:
- 120 ml icing sugar
- ½ teaspoon vanilla extract
- 2 to 3 tablespoons milk, whole or semi-skimmed
- Make the Apple Rolls

Instructions:

1. In a large bowl, whisk the flour, granulated sugar, and salt until blended. Stir in the butter and milk briefly until a sticky dough forms.
2. In a small bowl, stir together the brown sugar, cinnamon, and apple.
3. Place a piece of parchment paper on a work surface and dust it with flour. Roll the dough on the prepared surface to ¼ inch thickness.
4. Spread the apple mixture over the dough. Roll up the dough jelly roll-style, pinching the ends to seal. Cut the dough into 12 rolls.
5. Preheat the air fryer to 160°C.
6. Line the air fryer basket with parchment paper and spritz it with oil. Place 6 rolls on the prepared parchment.
7. Bake for 5 minutes. Flip the rolls and bake for 5 to 7 minutes more until lightly browned. Repeat with the remaining rolls. Make the Icing
8. In a medium bowl, whisk the icing sugar, vanilla, and milk until blended.
9. Drizzle over the warm rolls.

Homemade Toaster Pastries

Makes 6 pastries

Prep time: 10 minutes / Cook time: 11 minutes

Ingredients:
- Oil, for spraying
- 1 (425 g) package refrigerated piecrust
- 6 tablespoons jam or preserves of choice
- 475 ml icing sugar
- 3 tablespoons milk
- 1 to 2 tablespoons sprinkles of choice

Instructions:

1. Preheat the air fryer to 176°C. Line the air fryer basket with parchment and spray lightly with oil.
2. Cut the piecrust into 12 rectangles, about 3 by 4 inches each. You will need to reroll the dough scraps to get 12 rectangles.
3. Spread 1 tablespoon of jam in the center of 6 rectangles, leaving ¼ inch around the edges.
4. Pour some water into a small bowl. Use your finger to moisten the edge of each rectangle.
5. Top each rectangle with another and use your fingers to press around the edges. Using the tines of a fork, seal the edges of the dough and poke a few holes in the top of each one. Place the pastries in the prepared basket.
6. Air fry for 11 minutes. Let cool completely.
7. In a medium bowl, whisk together the icing sugar and milk. Spread the icing over the tops of the pastries and add sprinkles. Serve immediately.

Baked Peach Oatmeal

Serves 6

Prep time: 5 minutes / Cook time: 30 minutes

Ingredients:
- Olive oil cooking spray
- 475 ml certified gluten-free rolled oats
- 475 ml unsweetened almond milk
- 60 ml honey, plus more for drizzling (optional)
- 120 ml non-fat plain Greek yoghurt
- 1 teaspoon vanilla extract
- ½ teaspoon ground cinnamon
- ¼ teaspoon salt
- 350 ml diced peaches, divided, plus more for serving (optional)

Instructions:

1. Preheat the air fryer to 192°C. Lightly coat the inside of a 6-inch cake pan with olive oil cooking spray.
2. In a large bowl, mix together the oats, almond milk, honey, yoghurt, vanilla, cinnamon, and salt until well combined.
3. Fold in 180 ml peaches and then pour the mixture into the prepared cake pan.
4. Sprinkle the remaining peaches across the top of the oatmeal mixture. Bake in the air fryer for 30 minutes.
5. Allow to set and cool for 5 minutes before serving with additional fresh fruit and honey for drizzling, if desired.

Canadian Bacon Muffin Sandwiches

Serves 4

Prep time: 5 minutes / Cook time: 8 minutes

Ingredients:

- 4 English muffins, split
- 8 slices back bacon
- 4 slices cheese
- Cooking spray

Instructions:

1. Preheat the air fryer to 188°C.
2. Make the sandwiches: Top each of 4 muffin halves with 2 slices of bacon, 1 slice of cheese, and finish with the remaining muffin half.
3. Put the sandwiches in the air fryer basket and spritz the tops with cooking spray.
4. Bake for 4 minutes. Flip the sandwiches and bake for another 4 minutes.
5. Divide the sandwiches among four plates and serve warm.

Bacon, Cheese, and Avocado Melt

Serves 2

Prep time: 5 minutes / Cook time: 3 to 5 minutes

Ingredients:

- 1 avocado
- 4 slices cooked bacon, chopped
- 2 tablespoons salsa
- 1 tablespoon double cream
- 60 ml shredded Cheddar cheese

Instructions:

1. Preheat the air fryer to 204°C.
2. Slice the avocado in half lengthwise and remove the stone. To ensure the avocado halves do not roll in the basket, slice a thin piece of skin off the base.
3. In a small bowl, combine the bacon, salsa, and cream. Divide the mixture between the avocado halves and top with the cheese.
4. Place the avocado halves in the air fryer basket and air fry for 3 to 5 minutes until the cheese has melted and begins to brown. Serve warm.

Savory Sweet Potato Hash

Serves 6

Prep time: 15 minutes / Cook time: 18 minutes

Ingredients:

- 2 medium sweet potatoes, peeled and cut into 1-inch cubes
- ½ green pepper, diced
- ½ red onion, diced
- 110 g baby mushrooms, diced
- 2 tablespoons olive oil
- 1 garlic clove, minced
- ½ teaspoon salt
- ½ teaspoon black pepper
- ½ tablespoon chopped fresh rosemary

Instructions:

1. Preheat the air fryer to 192°C.
2. In a large bowl, toss all ingredients together until the vegetables are well coated and seasonings distributed.

3. Pour the vegetables into the air fryer basket, making sure they are in a single even layer. (If using a smaller air fryer, you may need to do this in two batches.)
4. Roast for 9 minutes, then toss or flip the vegetables. Roast for 9 minutes more.
5. Transfer to a serving bowl or individual plates and enjoy.

Cheddar Soufflés

Serves 4

Prep time: 15 minutes / Cook time: 12 minutes

Ingredients:

- 3 large eggs, whites and yolks separated
- ¼ teaspoon cream of tartar
- 120 ml shredded sharp Cheddar cheese
- 85 g cream cheese, softened

Instructions:

1. In a large bowl, beat egg whites together with cream of tartar until soft peaks form, about 2 minutes.
2. In a separate medium bowl, beat egg yolks, Cheddar, and cream cheese together until frothy, about 1 minute. Add egg yolk mixture to whites, gently folding until combined.
3. Pour mixture evenly into four ramekins greased with cooking spray. Place ramekins into air fryer basket. Adjust the temperature to 176°C and bake for 12 minutes. Eggs will be browned on the top and firm in the center when done. Serve warm.

Breakfast Pitta

Serves 2

Prep time: 5 minutes / Cook time: 6 minutes

Ingredients:

- 1 wholemeal pitta
- 2 teaspoons olive oil
- ½ shallot, diced

- ¼ teaspoon garlic, minced
- 1 large egg
- ¼ teaspoon dried oregano
- ¼ teaspoon dried thyme
- ⅛ teaspoon salt
- 2 tablespoons shredded Parmesan cheese

Instructions:

1. Preheat the air fryer to 192°C.
2. Brush the top of the pitta with olive oil, then spread the diced shallot and minced garlic over the pitta.
3. Crack the egg into a small bowl or ramekin, and season it with oregano, thyme, and salt.
4. Place the pitta into the air fryer basket, and gently pour the egg onto the top of the pitta. Sprinkle with cheese over the top.
5. Bake for 6 minutes.
6. Allow to cool for 5 minutes before cutting into pieces for serving.

Turkey Breakfast Sausage Patties

Serves 4

Prep time: 5 minutes / Cook time: 10 minutes

Ingredients:

- 1 tablespoon chopped fresh thyme
- 1 tablespoon chopped fresh sage
- 1¼ teaspoons coarse or flaky salt
- 1 teaspoon chopped fennel seeds
- ¾ teaspoon smoked paprika
- ½ teaspoon onion granules
- ½ teaspoon garlic powder
- ⅛ teaspoon crushed red pepper flakes
- ⅛ teaspoon freshly ground black pepper
- 450 g lean turkey mince
- 120 ml finely minced sweet apple (peeled)

Instructions:

1. Thoroughly combine the thyme, sage, salt, fennel seeds, paprika, onion granules, garlic powder, red pepper flakes, and black pepper

in a medium bowl.

2. Add the turkey mince and apple and stir until well incorporated. Divide the mixture into 8 equal portions and shape into patties with your hands, each about ¼ inch thick and 3 inches in diameter.

3. Preheat the air fryer to 204ºC.

4. Place the patties in the air fryer basket in a single layer. You may need to work in batches to avoid overcrowding.

5. Air fry for 5 minutes. Flip the patties and air fry for 5 minutes, or until the patties are nicely browned and cooked through.

6. Remove from the basket to a plate and repeat with the remaining patties.

7. Serve warm.

Veggie Frittata

Serves 2

Prep time: 7 minutes / Cook time: 21 to 23 minutes

Ingredients:

- Avocado oil spray
- 60 ml diced red onion
- 60 ml diced red pepper
- 60 ml finely chopped broccoli
- 4 large eggs
- 85 g shredded sharp Cheddar cheese, divided
- ½ teaspoon dried thyme
- Sea salt and freshly ground black pepper, to taste

Instructions:

1. Spray a pan well with oil. Put the onion, pepper, and broccoli in the pan, place the pan in the air fryer, and set to 176ºC. Bake for 5 minutes.

2. While the vegetables cook, beat the eggs in a medium bowl. Stir in half of the cheese, and season with the thyme, salt, and pepper.

3. Add the eggs to the pan and top with the remaining cheese. Set the air fryer to 176ºC. Bake for 16 to 18 minutes, until cooked through.

Kale and Potato Nuggets

Serves 4

Prep time: 10 minutes / Cook time: 18 minutes

Ingredients:

- 1 teaspoon extra virgin olive oil
- 1 clove garlic, minced
- 1 L kale, rinsed and chopped
- 475 ml potatoes, boiled and mashed
- 30 ml milk
- Salt and ground black pepper, to taste
- Cooking spray

Instructions:

1. Preheat the air fryer to 200ºC.

2. In a skillet over medium heat, sauté the garlic in the olive oil, until it turns golden brown. Sauté with the kale for an additional 3 minutes and remove from the heat.

3. Mix the mashed potatoes, kale and garlic in a bowl. Pour in the milk and sprinkle with salt and pepper.

4. Shape the mixture into nuggets and spritz with cooking spray.

5. Put in the air fryer basket and air fry for 15 minutes, flip the nuggets halfway through cooking to make sure the nuggets fry evenly.

6. Serve immediately.

Everything Bagels

Makes 6 bagels

Prep time: 15 minutes / Cook time: 14 minutes

Ingredients:

- 415 ml shredded Mozzarella cheese or goat cheese Mozzarella
- 2 tablespoons unsalted butter or coconut oil
- 1 large egg, beaten
- 1 tablespoon apple cider vinegar
- 235 ml blanched almond flour
- 1 tablespoon baking powder
- ⅛ teaspoon fine sea salt

- 1½ teaspoons sesame seeds or za'atar

Instructions:

1. Make the dough: Put the Mozzarella and butter in a large microwave-safe bowl and microwave for 1 to 2 minutes, until the cheese is entirely melted. Stir well. Add the egg and vinegar. Using a hand mixer on medium, combine well. Add the almond flour, baking powder, and salt and, using the mixer, combine well.

2. Lay a piece of parchment paper on the countertop and place the dough on it. Knead it for about 3 minutes. The dough should be a little sticky but pliable. (If the dough is too sticky, chill it in the refrigerator for an hour or overnight.)

3. Preheat the air fryer to 176°C. Spray a baking sheet or pie pan that will fit into your air fryer with avocado oil.

4. Divide the dough into 6 equal portions. Roll 1 portion into a log that is 6 inches long and about ½ inch thick. Form the log into a circle and seal the edges together, making a bagel shape. Repeat with the remaining portions of dough, making 6 bagels.

5. Place the bagels on the greased baking sheet. Spray the bagels with avocado oil and top with everything bagel seasoning, pressing the seasoning into the dough with your hands.

6. Place the bagels in the air fryer and bake for 14 minutes, or until cooked through and golden brown, flipping after 6 minutes.

7. Remove the bagels from the air fryer and allow them to cool slightly before slicing them in half and serving. Store leftovers in an airtight container in the fridge for up to 4 days or in the freezer for up to a month.

Easy Sausage Pizza

Serves 4

Prep time: 10 minutes / Cook time: 6 minutes

Ingredients:

- 2 tablespoons ketchup
- 1 pitta bread
- 80 ml sausage meat
- 230 g Mozzarella cheese
- 1 teaspoon garlic powder
- 1 tablespoon olive oil

Instructions:

1. Preheat the air fryer to 172°C.
2. Spread the ketchup over the pitta bread.
3. Top with the sausage meat and cheese. Sprinkle with the garlic powder and olive oil.
4. Put the pizza in the air fryer basket and bake for 6 minutes.
5. Serve warm.

Denver Omelette

Serves 1

Prep time: 5 minutes / Cook time: 8 minutes

Ingredients:

- 2 large eggs
- 60 ml unsweetened, unflavoured almond milk
- ¼ teaspoon fine sea salt
- ⅛ teaspoon ground black pepper
- 60 ml diced ham (omit for vegetarian)
- 60 ml diced green and red peppers
- 2 tablespoons diced spring onions, plus more for garnish
- 60 ml shredded Cheddar cheese (about 30 g) (omit for dairy-free)
- Quartered cherry tomatoes, for serving (optional)

Instructions:

1. Preheat the air fryer to 176°C. Grease a cake pan and set aside.
2. In a small bowl, use a fork to whisk together the eggs, almond milk, salt, and pepper. Add the ham, peppers, and spring onions. Pour the mixture into the greased pan. Add the

cheese on top (if using).

3. Place the pan in the basket of the air fryer. Bake for 8 minutes, or until the eggs are cooked to your liking.

4. Loosen the omelette from the sides of the pan with a spatula and place it on a serving plate. Garnish with spring onions and serve with cherry tomatoes, if desired. Best served fresh.

Cinnamon Rolls

Makes 12 rolls

Prep time: 10 minutes / Cook time: 20 minutes

Ingredients:

- 600 ml shredded Mozzarella cheese
- 60 g cream cheese, softened
- 235 ml blanched finely ground almond flour
- ½ teaspoon vanilla extract
- 120 ml icing sugar-style sweetener
- 1 tablespoon ground cinnamon

Instructions:

1. In a large microwave-safe bowl, combine Mozzarella cheese, cream cheese, and flour. Microwave the mixture on high 90 seconds until cheese is melted.

2. Add vanilla extract and sweetener, and mix 2 minutes until a dough forms.

3. Once the dough is cool enough to work with your hands, about 2 minutes, spread it out into a 12 × 4-inch rectangle on ungreased parchment paper. Evenly sprinkle dough with cinnamon.

4. Starting at the long side of the dough, roll lengthwise to form a log. Slice the log into twelve even pieces.

5. Divide rolls between two ungreased round nonstick baking dishes. Place one dish into air fryer basket. Adjust the temperature to 192°C and bake for 10 minutes.

6. Cinnamon rolls will be done when golden around the edges and mostly firm. Repeat with second dish. Allow rolls to cool in dishes 10 minutes before serving.

Sausage Stuffed Peppers

Serves 4

Prep time: 15 minutes / Cook time: 15 minutes

Ingredients:

- 230 g spicy pork sausage meat, removed from casings
- 4 large eggs
- 110 g full-fat cream cheese, softened
- 60 ml tinned diced tomatoes, drained
- 4 green peppers
- 8 tablespoons shredded chilli cheese
- 120 ml full-fat sour cream

Instructions:

1. In a medium skillet over medium heat, crumble and brown the sausage meat until no pink remains. Remove sausage and drain the fat from the pan. Crack eggs into the pan, scramble, and cook until no longer runny.

2. Place cooked sausage in a large bowl and fold in cream cheese. Mix in diced tomatoes. Gently fold in eggs.

3. Cut a 4-inch to 5-inch slit in the top of each pepper, removing the seeds and white membrane with a small knife. Separate the filling into four servings and spoon carefully into each pepper. Top each with 2 tablespoons cheese.

4. Place each pepper into the air fryer basket.

5. Adjust the temperature to 176°C and set the timer for 15 minutes.

6. Peppers will be soft and cheese will be browned when ready. Serve immediately with sour cream on top.

Cajun Shrimp

Serves 4

Prep time: 15 minutes / Cook time: 9 minutes

Ingredients:
- Oil, for spraying
- 450 g jumbo raw shrimp, peeled and deveined
- 1 tablespoon Cajun seasoning
- 170 g cooked kielbasa, cut into thick slices
- ½ medium courgette, cut into ¼-inch-thick slices
- ½ medium yellow squash or butternut squash, cut into ¼-inch-thick slices
- 1 green pepper, seeded and cut into 1-inch pieces
- 2 tablespoons olive oil
- ½ teaspoon salt

Instructions:
1. Preheat the air fryer to 204°C.
2. Line the air fryer basket with parchment and spray lightly with oil. In a large bowl, toss together the shrimp and Cajun seasoning.
3. Add the kielbasa, courgette, squash, pepper, olive oil, and salt and mix well.
4. Transfer the mixture to the prepared basket, taking care not to overcrowd.
5. You may need to work in batches, depending on the size of your air fryer.
6. Cook for 9 minutes, shaking and stirring every 3 minutes.
7. Serve immediately.

Veggie Tuna Melts

Serves 4

Prep time: 15 minutes / Cook time: 7 to 11 minutes

Ingredients:
- 2 low-salt wholemeal English muffins, split
- 1 (170 g) can chunk light low-salt tuna, drained
- 235 ml shredded carrot
- 80 ml chopped mushrooms
- 2 spring onions, white and green parts, sliced
- 80 ml fat-free Greek yoghurt
- 2 tablespoons low-salt wholegrain mustard
- 2 slices low-salt low-fat Swiss cheese, halved

Instructions:
1. Place the English muffin halves in the air fryer basket.
2. Air fry at 172°C for 3 to 4 minutes, or until crisp.
3. Remove from the basket and set aside. In a medium bowl, thoroughly mix the tuna, carrot, mushrooms, spring onions, yoghurt, and mustard.
4. Top each half of the muffins with one-fourth of the tuna mixture and a half slice of Swiss cheese.
5. Air fry for 4 to 7 minutes, or until the tuna mixture is hot and the cheese melts and starts to brown.
6. Serve immediately.

Pork Burgers with Red Cabbage Salad

Serves 4

Prep time: 20 minutes / Cook time: 7 to 9 minutes

Ingredients:
- 120 ml Greek yoghurt
- 2 tablespoons low-salt mustard, divided
- 1 tablespoon lemon juice
- 60 ml sliced red cabbage
- 60 ml grated carrots
- 450 g lean minced pork
- ½ teaspoon paprika
- 235 ml mixed baby lettuce greens
- 2 small tomatoes, sliced
- 8 small low-salt wholemeal sandwich buns, cut in half

Instructions:
1. In a small bowl, combine the yoghurt, 1 tablespoon mustard, lemon juice, cabbage, and carrots; mix and refrigerate.
2. In a medium bowl, combine the pork,

remaining 1 tablespoon mustard, and paprika.

3. Form into 8 small patties. Put the sliders into the air fryer basket.
4. Air fry at 204°C for 7 to 9 minutes, or until the sliders register 74°C as tested with a meat thermometer.
5. Assemble the burgers by placing some of the lettuce greens on a bun bottom.
6. Top with a tomato slice, the burgers, and the cabbage mixture.
7. Add the bun top and serve immediately.

Air Fryer Homemade Croutons

Serves: 4
Prep Time: 5 minutes/Cook Time: 8 minutes

Ingredients:
- 4 slices of bread, cut into cubes
- 1 tbsp (15ml) olive oil
¼ tsp (**Instructions:**
- 1. 25ml) garlic powder
¼ tsp (**Instructions:**
- 1. 25ml) onion powder
- Salt and pepper, to taste

Instructions:
1. Preheat your air fryer to 180°C.
2. In a large bowl, toss the bread cubes with olive oil, garlic powder, onion powder, salt, and pepper.
3. Place the bread cubes in the air fryer basket in a single layer.
4. Air fry for 8 minutes or until the croutons are golden brown and crispy.
5. Once the croutons are done, remove them from the air fryer and allow them to cool before serving.
6. Store any leftover croutons in an airtight container for up to 3 days.

Filo Vegetable Triangles

Serves 6
Prep time: 15 minutes / Cook time: 6 to 11 minutes

Ingredients:
- 3 tablespoons minced onion
- 2 garlic cloves, minced
- 2 tablespoons grated carrot
- 1 teaspoon olive oil
- 3 tablespoons frozen baby peas, thawed
- 2 tablespoons fat-free soft white cheese, at room temperature
- 6 sheets frozen filo pastry, thawed
- Olive oil spray, for coating the dough

Instructions:
1. In a baking pan, combine the onion, garlic, carrot, and olive oil.
2. Air fry at 200°C for 2 to 4 minutes, or until the vegetables are crisp-tender. Transfer to a bowl. Stir in the peas and soft white cheese to the vegetable mixture.
3. Let cool while you prepare the dough. Lay one sheet of filo on a work surface and lightly spray with olive oil spray.
4. Top with another sheet of filo. Repeat with the remaining 4 filo sheets; you'll have 3 stacks with 2 layers each.
5. Cut each stack lengthwise into 4 strips (12 strips total).
6. Place a scant 2 teaspoons of the filling near the bottom of each strip.
7. Bring one corner up over the filling to make a triangle; continue folding the triangles over, as you would fold a flag.
8. Seal the edge with a bit of water.
9. Repeat with the remaining strips and filling.
10. Air fry the triangles, in 2 batches, for 4 to 7 minutes, or until golden brown. Serve.

Beef Bratwursts

Serves 4
Prep time: 5 minutes / Cook time: 15 minutes

Ingredients:
- 4 (85 g) beef bratwursts

Instructions:
1. Preheat the air fryer to 192°C.

2. Place the beef bratwursts in the air fryer basket and air fry for 15 minutes, turning once halfway through.
3. Serve hot.

Bacon Pinwheels

Makes 8 pinwheels
Prep time: 10 minutes / Cook time: 10 minutes

Ingredients:

- 1 sheet puff pastry
- 2 tablespoons maple syrup
- 60 ml brown sugar
- 8 slices bacon
- Ground black pepper, to taste
- Cooking spray

Instructions:

1. Preheat the air fryer to 182°C.
2. Spritz the air fryer basket with cooking spray.
3. Roll the puff pastry into a 10-inch square with a rolling pin on a clean work surface, then cut the pastry into 8 strips.
4. Brush the strips with maple syrup and sprinkle with sugar, leaving a 1-inch far end uncovered.
5. Arrange each slice of bacon on each strip, leaving a ⅛-inch length of bacon hang over the end close to you.
6. Sprinkle with black pepper. From the end close to you, roll the strips into pinwheels, then dab the uncovered end with water and seal the rolls.
7. Arrange the pinwheels in the preheated air fryer and spritz with cooking spray.
8. Air fry for 10 minutes or until golden brown.
9. Flip the pinwheels halfway through.
10. Serve immediately.

Easy Devils on Horseback

Serves 12
Prep time: 5 minutes / Cook time: 7 minutes

Ingredients:

- 24 small pitted prunes (128 g)
- 60 ml crumbled blue cheese, divided
- 8 slices centre-cut bacon, cut crosswise into thirds

Instructions:

1. Preheat the air fryer to 204°C.
2. Halve the prunes lengthwise, but don't cut them all the way through.
3. Place ½ teaspoon of cheese in the centre of each prune.
4. Wrap a piece of bacon around each prune and secure the bacon with a toothpick.
5. Working in batches, arrange a single layer of the prunes in the air fryer basket.
6. Air fry for about 7 minutes, flipping halfway, until the bacon is cooked through and crisp.
7. Let cool slightly and serve warm.

Beery and Crunchy Onion Rings

Serves 2 to 4
Prep time: 10 minutes / Cook time: 16 minutes

Ingredients:

- 160 ml plain flour
- 1 teaspoon paprika
- ½ teaspoon bicarbonate of soda
- 1 teaspoon salt
- ½ teaspoon freshly ground black pepper
- 1 egg, beaten
- 180 ml beer
- 350 ml breadcrumbs
- 1 tablespoons olive oil
- 1 large Vidalia or sweet onion, peeled and sliced into ½-inch rings
- Cooking spray

Instructions:

1. Preheat the air fryer to 182°C.
2. Spritz the air fryer basket with cooking spray. Combine the flour, paprika, bicarbonate of soda, salt, and ground black pepper in a bowl.

3. Stir to mix well. Combine the egg and beer in a separate bowl. Stir to mix well.
4. Make a well in the centre of the flour mixture, then pour the egg mixture in the well. Stir to mix everything well.
5. Pour the breadcrumbs and olive oil in a shallow plate. Stir to mix well.
6. Dredge the onion rings gently into the flour and egg mixture, then shake the excess off and put into the plate of breadcrumbs.
7. Flip to coat both sides well. Arrange the onion rings in the preheated air fryer.
8. Air fry in batches for 16 minutes or until golden brown and crunchy.
9. Flip the rings and put the bottom rings to the top halfway through.
10. Serve immediately.

Simple Pea Delight

Serves 2 to 4

Prep time: 5 minutes / Cook time: 15 minutes

Ingredients:
- 235 ml flour
- 1 teaspoon baking powder
- 3 eggs
- 235 ml coconut milk
- 235 ml soft white cheese
- 3 tablespoons pea protein
- 120 ml chicken or turkey strips
- Pinch of sea salt
- 235 ml Mozzarella cheese

Instructions:
1. Preheat the air fryer to 200ºC.
2. In a large bowl, mix all ingredients together using a large wooden spoon.
3. Spoon equal amounts of the mixture into muffin cups and bake for 15 minutes.
4. Serve immediately.

Scalloped Veggie Mix

Serves 4

Prep time: 10 minutes / Cook time: 15 minutes

Ingredients:
- 1 Yukon Gold or other small white potato, thinly sliced
- 1 small sweet potato, peeled and thinly sliced
- 1 medium carrot, thinly sliced
- 60 ml minced onion
- 3 garlic cloves, minced
- 180 ml 2 percent milk
- 2 tablespoons cornflour
- ½ teaspoon dried thyme

Instructions:
1. Preheat the air fryer to 192ºC. In a baking pan, layer the potato, sweet potato, carrot, onion, and garlic.
2. In a small bowl, whisk the milk, cornflour, and thyme until blended.
3. Pour the milk mixture evenly over the vegetables in the pan.
4. Bake for 15 minutes. Check the casserole—it should be golden brown on top, and the vegetables should be tender.
5. Serve immediately.

Cheesy Jalapeño Cornbread

Prep timeCheesy Jalapeño Cornbread

Ingredients:
- 160 ml cornmeal
- 80 ml plain flour
- ¾ teaspoon baking powder
- 2 tablespoons margarine, melted
- ½ teaspoon rock salt
- 1 tablespoon granulated sugar
- 180 ml whole milk
- 1 large egg, beaten
- 1 jalapeño pepper, thinly sliced
- 80 ml shredded extra mature Cheddar cheese
- Cooking spray

Instructions:
1. Preheat the air fryer to 152ºC.
2. Spritz the air fryer basket with cooking spray.

3. Combine all the ingredients in a large bowl. Stir to mix well.
4. Pour the mixture in a baking pan.
5. Arrange the pan in the preheated air fryer. Bake for 20 minutes or until a toothpick inserted in the centre of the bread comes out clean.
6. When the cooking is complete, remove the baking pan from the air fryer and allow the bread to cool for a few minutes before slicing to serve.

Cheesy Potato Patties

Serves 8

Prep time: 5 minutes / Cook time: 10 minutes

Ingredients:
- 900 g white potatoes
- 120 ml finely chopped spring onions
- ½ teaspoon freshly ground black pepper, or more to taste
- 1 tablespoon fine sea salt
- ½ teaspoon hot paprika
- 475 ml shredded Colby or Monterey Jack cheese
- 60 ml rapeseed oil
- 235 ml crushed crackers

Instructions:
1. Preheat the air fryer to 182°C. Boil the potatoes until soft.
2. Dry them off and peel them before mashing thoroughly, leaving no lumps.
3. Combine the mashed potatoes with spring onions, pepper, salt, paprika, and cheese.
4. Mould the mixture into balls with your hands and press with your palm to flatten them into patties.
5. In a shallow dish, combine the rapeseed oil and crushed crackers. Coat the patties in the crumb mixture.
6. Bake the patties for about 10 minutes, in multiple batches if necessary. Serve hot.

Easy Roasted Asparagus

Serves 4

Prep time: 5 minutes / Cook time: 6 minutes

Ingredients:
- 450 g asparagus, trimmed and halved crosswise
- 1 teaspoon extra-virgin olive oil
- Salt and pepper, to taste
- Lemon wedges, for serving

Instructions:
1. Preheat the air fryer to 204°C.
2. Toss the asparagus with the oil, ⅛ teaspoon salt, and ⅛ teaspoon pepper in bowl. Transfer to air fryer basket.
3. Place the basket in air fryer and roast for 6 to 8 minutes, or until tender and bright green, tossing halfway through cooking.
4. Season with salt and pepper and serve with lemon wedges.

Herb-Roasted Veggies

Serves 4

Prep time: 10 minutes / Cook time: 14 to 18 minutes

Ingredients:
- 1 red pepper, sliced
- 1 (230 g) package sliced mushrooms
- 235 ml green beans, cut into 2-inch pieces
- 80 ml diced red onion
- 3 garlic cloves, sliced
- 1 teaspoon olive oil
- ½ teaspoon dried basil
- ½ teaspoon dried tarragon

Instructions:
1. Preheat the air fryer to 176°C.
2. In a medium bowl, mix the red pepper, mushrooms, green beans, red onion, and garlic.
3. Drizzle with the olive oil. Toss to coat.
4. Add the herbs and toss again.
5. Place the vegetables in the air fryer basket. Roast for 14 to 18 minutes, or until tender.
6. Serve immediately.

French Garlic Chicken

Serves 4

Prep time: 30 minutes / Cook time: 27 minutes

Ingredients:

- 2 tablespoon extra-virgin olive oil
- 1 tablespoon Dijon mustard
- 1 tablespoon apple cider vinegar
- 3 cloves garlic, minced
- 2 teaspoons herbes de Provence
- ½ teaspoon kosher salt
- 1 teaspoon black pepper
- 450 g boneless, skinless chicken thighs, halved crosswise
- 2 tablespoons butter
- 8 cloves garlic, chopped
- 60 g heavy whipping cream

Instructions:

1. In a small bowl, combine the olive oil, mustard, vinegar, minced garlic, herbes de Provence, salt, and pepper. Use a wire whisk to emulsify the mixture.
2. Pierce the chicken all over with a fork to allow the marinade to penetrate better. Place the chicken in a resealable plastic bag, pour the marinade over, and seal. Massage until the chicken is well coated. Marinate at room temperature for 30 minutes or in the refrigerator for up to 24 hours.
3. When you are ready to cook, place the butter and chopped garlic in a baking pan and place it in the air fryer basket. Set the air fryer to 200ºC for 5 minutes, or until the butter has melted and the garlic is sizzling.
4. Add the chicken and the marinade to the seasoned butter. Set the air fryer to 180ºC for 15 minutes. Use a meat thermometer to ensure the chicken has reached an internal temperature of 76ºC. Transfer the chicken to a plate and cover lightly with foil to keep warm.
5. Add the cream to the pan, stirring to combine with the garlic, butter, and cooking juices. Place the pan in the air fryer basket. Set the air fryer to 180ºC for 7 minutes.
6. Pour the thickened sauce over the chicken and serve.

Breaded Turkey Cutlets

Serves 4

Prep time: 5 minutes / Cook time: 8 minutes

Ingredients:

- 60 g whole wheat bread crumbs
- ¼ teaspoon paprika
- ¼ teaspoon salt
- ¼ teaspoon black pepper
- ⅛ teaspoon dried sage
- ⅛ teaspoon garlic powder
- 1 egg
- 4 turkey breast cutlets
- Chopped fresh parsley, for serving

Instructions:

1. Preheat the air fryer to 192ºC.
2. In a medium shallow bowl, whisk together the bread crumbs, paprika, salt, black pepper, sage, and garlic powder.
3. In a separate medium shallow bowl, whisk the egg until frothy.
4. Dip each turkey cutlet into the egg mixture, then into the bread crumb mixture, coating the outside with the crumbs. Place the breaded turkey cutlets in a single layer in the bottom of the air fryer basket, making sure

that they don't touch each other.

5. Bake for 4 minutes. Turn the cutlets over, then bake for 4 minutes more, or until the internal temperature reaches 76°C. Sprinkle on the parsley and serve.

Chicken Chimichangas

Serves 4

Prep time: 20 minutes / Cook time: 8 to 10 minutes

Ingredients:

- 280 g cooked chicken, shredded
- 2 tablespoons chopped green chilies
- ½ teaspoon oregano
- ½ teaspoon cumin
- ½ teaspoon onion powder
- ¼ teaspoon garlic powder
- Salt and pepper, to taste
- 8 flour tortillas (6- or 7-inch diameter)
- Oil for misting or cooking spray
- Chimichanga Sauce:
- 2 tablespoons butter
- 2 tablespoons flour
- 235 ml chicken broth
- 60 g light sour cream
- ¼ teaspoon salt
- 60 g Pepper Jack or Monterey Jack cheese, shredded

Instructions:

1. Make the sauce by melting butter in a saucepan over medium-low heat. Stir in flour until smooth and slightly bubbly. Gradually add broth, stirring constantly until smooth. Cook and stir 1 minute, until the mixture slightly thickens. Remove from heat and stir in sour cream and salt. Set aside.

2. In a medium bowl, mix together the chicken, chilies, oregano, cumin, onion powder, garlic, salt, and pepper. Stir in 3 to 4 tablespoons of the sauce, using just enough to make the filling moist but not soupy.

3. Divide filling among the 8 tortillas. Place filling down the centre of tortilla, stopping about 1 inch from edges. Fold one side of tortilla over filling, fold the two sides in, and then roll up. Mist all sides with oil or cooking spray.

4. Place chimichangas in air fryer basket seam side down. To fit more into the basket, you can stand them on their sides with the seams against the sides of the basket.

5. Air fry at 180°C for 8 to 10 minutes or until heated through and crispy brown outside.

6. Add the shredded cheese to the remaining sauce. Stir over low heat, warming just until the cheese melts. Don't boil or sour cream may curdle.

7. Drizzle the sauce over the chimichangas.

Thanksgiving Turkey Breast

Serves 4

Prep time: 5 minutes / Cook time: 30 minutes

Ingredients:

- 1½ teaspoons fine sea salt
- 1 teaspoon ground black pepper
- 1 teaspoon chopped fresh rosemary leaves
- 1 teaspoon chopped fresh sage
- 1 teaspoon chopped fresh tarragon
- 1 teaspoon chopped fresh thyme leaves
- 1 (900 g) turkey breast
- 3 tablespoons ghee or unsalted butter, melted
- 3 tablespoons Dijon mustard

Instructions:

1. Spray the air fryer with avocado oil. Preheat the air fryer to 200°C.

2. In a small bowl, stir together the salt, pepper, and herbs until well combined. Season the turkey breast generously on all sides with the seasoning.

3. In another small bowl, stir together the ghee and Dijon. Brush the ghee mixture on all sides of the turkey breast.

4. Place the turkey breast in the air fryer basket and air fry for 30 minutes, or until the internal temperature reaches 76°C. Transfer the breast to a cutting board and allow it to rest for 10 minutes before cutting it into ½-inch-thick slices.

5. Store leftovers in an airtight container in the refrigerator for up to 4 days or in the freezer for up to a month. Reheat in a preheated 180°C air fryer for 4 minutes, or until warmed through.

Thai Tacos with Peanut Sauce

Serves 4

Prep time: 10 minutes / Cook time: 6 minutes

Ingredients:

- 450 g chicken mince
- 10 g diced onions (about 1 small onion)
- 2 cloves garlic, minced
- ¼ teaspoon fine sea salt
- Sauce:
- 60 g creamy peanut butter, room temperature
- 2 tablespoons chicken broth, plus more if needed
- 2 tablespoons lime juice
- 2 tablespoons grated fresh ginger
- 2 tablespoons wheat-free tamari or coconut aminos
- 1½ teaspoons hot sauce
- 5 drops liquid stevia (optional)
- For Serving:
- 2 small heads butter lettuce, leaves separated
- Lime slices (optional)
- For Garnish (Optional):
- Coriander leaves
- Shredded purple cabbage
- Sliced green onions

Instructions:

1. Preheat the air fryer to 180°C. .

2. Place the chicken mince, onions, garlic, and salt in a pie pan or a dish that will fit in your air fryer. Break up the chicken with a spatula. Place in the air fryer and bake for 5 minutes, or until the chicken is browned and cooked through. Break up the chicken again into small crumbles.

3. Make the sauce: In a medium-sized bowl, stir together the peanut butter, broth, lime juice, ginger, tamari, hot sauce, and stevia (if using) until well combined. If the sauce is too thick, add another tablespoon or two of broth. Taste and add more hot sauce if desired.

4. Add half of the sauce to the pan with the chicken. Cook for another minute, until heated through, and stir well to combine.

5. Assemble the tacos: Place several lettuce leaves on a serving plate. Place a few tablespoons of the chicken mixture in each lettuce leaf and garnish with coriander leaves, purple cabbage, and sliced green onions, if desired. Serve the remaining sauce on the side. Serve with lime slices, if desired.

6. Store leftover meat mixture in an airtight container in the refrigerator for up to 4 days; store leftover sauce, lettuce leaves, and garnishes separately. Reheat the meat mixture in a lightly greased pie pan in a preheated 180°C air fryer for 3 minutes, or until heated through.

Peachy Chicken Chunks with Cherries

Serves 4

Prep time: 8 minutes / Cook time: 14 to 16 minutes

Ingredients:

- 100 g peach preserves

- 1 teaspoon ground rosemary
- ½ teaspoon black pepper
- ½ teaspoon salt
- ½ teaspoon marjoram
- 1 teaspoon light olive oil
- 450 g boneless chicken breasts, cut in 1½-inch chunks
- Oil for misting or cooking spray
- 1 (280 g) package frozen unsweetened dark cherries, thawed and drained

Instructions:

1. In a medium bowl, mix together peach preserves, rosemary, pepper, salt, marjoram, and olive oil.
2. Stir in chicken chunks and toss to coat well with the preserve mixture.
3. Spray the air fryer basket with oil or cooking spray and lay chicken chunks in basket.
4. Air fry at 200°C for 7 minutes. Stir. Cook for 6 to 8 more minutes or until chicken juices run clear.
5. When chicken has cooked through, scatter the cherries over and cook for additional minute to heat cherries.

Turkey and Cranberry Quesadillas

Serves 4

Prep time: 7 minutes / Cook time: 4 to 8 minutes

Ingredients:

- 6 low-sodium whole-wheat tortillas
- 75 g shredded low-sodium low-fat Swiss cheese
- 105 g shredded cooked low-sodium turkey breast
- 2 tablespoons cranberry sauce
- 2 tablespoons dried cranberries
- ½ teaspoon dried basil
- Olive oil spray, for spraying the tortillas

Instructions:

1. Preheat the air fryer to 200°C.
2. Put 3 tortillas on a work surface.
3. Evenly divide the Swiss cheese, turkey, cranberry sauce, and dried cranberries among the tortillas. Sprinkle with the basil and top with the remaining tortillas.
4. Spray the outsides of the tortillas with olive oil spray.
5. One at a time, air fry the quesadillas in the air fryer for 4 to 8 minutes, or until crisp and the cheese is melted. Cut into quarters and serve.

Fajita Chicken Strips

Serves 4

Prep time: 10 minutes / Cook time: 15 minutes

Ingredients:

- 450 g boneless, skinless chicken tenderloins, cut into strips
- 3 bell peppers, any color, cut into chunks
- 1 onion, cut into chunks
- 1 tablespoon olive oil
- 1 tablespoon fajita seasoning mix
- Cooking spray

Instructions:

1. Preheat the air fryer to 190°C.
2. In a large bowl, mix together the chicken, bell peppers, onion, olive oil, and fajita seasoning mix until completely coated.
3. Spray the air fryer basket lightly with cooking spray.
4. Place the chicken and vegetables in the air fryer basket and lightly spray with cooking spray.
5. Air fry for 7 minutes. Shake the basket and air fry for an additional 5 to 8 minutes, until the chicken is cooked through and the veggies are starting to char.
6. Serve warm.

Chicken Legs with Leeks

Serves 6

Prep time: 30 minutes / Cook time: 18 minutes

Ingredients:

- 2 leeks, sliced
- 2 large-sized tomatoes, chopped
- 3 cloves garlic, minced
- ½ teaspoon dried oregano
- 6 chicken legs, boneless and skinless
- ½ teaspoon smoked cayenne pepper
- 2 tablespoons olive oil
- A freshly ground nutmeg

Instructions:

1. In a mixing dish, thoroughly combine all ingredients, minus the leeks. Place in the refrigerator and let it marinate overnight.
2. Lay the leeks onto the bottom of the air fryer basket. Top with the chicken legs.
3. Roast chicken legs at (190ºC for 18 minutes, turning halfway through. Serve with hoisin sauce.

Classic Chicken Kebab

Serves 4

Prep time: 35 minutes / Cook time: 25 minutes

Ingredients:

- 60 ml olive oil
- 1 teaspoon garlic powder
- 1 teaspoon onion powder
- 1 teaspoon ground cumin
- ½ teaspoon dried oregano
- ½ teaspoon dried basil
- 60 ml lemon juice
- 1 tablespoon apple cider vinegar
- Olive oil cooking spray
- 450 g boneless skinless chicken thighs, cut into 1-inch pieces
- 1 red bell pepper, cut into 1-inch pieces
- 1 red onion, cut into 1-inch pieces
- 1 courgette, cut into 1-inch pieces
- 12 cherry tomatoes

Instructions:

1. In a large bowl, mix together the olive oil, garlic powder, onion powder, cumin, oregano, basil, lemon juice, and apple cider vinegar.
2. Spray six skewers with olive oil cooking spray.
3. On each skewer, slide on a piece of chicken, then a piece of bell pepper, onion, courgette, and finally a tomato and then repeat. Each skewer should have at least two pieces of each item.
4. Once all of the skewers are prepared, place them in a 9-by-13-inch baking dish and pour the olive oil marinade over the top of the skewers. Turn each skewer so that all sides of the chicken and vegetables are coated.
5. Cover the dish with plastic wrap and place it in the refrigerator for 30 minutes.
6. After 30 minutes, preheat the air fryer to 192ºC. (If using a grill attachment, make sure it is inside the air fryer during preheating.)
7. Remove the skewers from the marinade and lay them in a single layer in the air fryer basket. If the air fryer has a grill attachment, you can also lay them on this instead.
8. Cook for 10 minutes. Rotate the kebabs, then cook them for 15 minutes more.
9. Remove the skewers from the air fryer and let them rest for 5 minutes before serving.

Pork Rind Fried Chicken

Serves 4

Prep time: 30 minutes / Cook time: 20 minutes

Ingredients:

- 60 ml buffalo sauce
- 4 (115 g) boneless, skinless chicken breasts
- ½ teaspoon paprika
- ½ teaspoon garlic powder
- ¼ teaspoon ground black pepper
- 60 g g plain pork rinds, finely crushed

Instructions:

1. Pour buffalo sauce into a large sealable bowl or bag. Add chicken and toss to coat. Place sealed bowl or bag into refrigerator and let marinate at least 30 minutes up to overnight.
2. Remove chicken from marinade but do not shake excess sauce off chicken. Sprinkle both sides of thighs with paprika, garlic powder, and pepper.
3. Place pork rinds into a large bowl and press each chicken breast into pork rinds to coat evenly on both sides.
4. Place chicken into ungreased air fryer basket. Adjust the temperature to 200°C and roast for 20 minutes, turning chicken halfway through cooking. Chicken will be golden and have an internal temperature of at least 76°C when done. Serve warm.

Chicken with Lettuce

Serves 4

Prep time: 15 minutes / Cook time: 14 minutes

Ingredients:

- 450 g chicken breast tenders, chopped into bite-size pieces
- ½ onion, thinly sliced
- ½ red bell pepper, seeded and thinly sliced
- ½ green bell pepper, seeded and thinly sliced
- 1 tablespoon olive oil
- 1 tablespoon fajita seasoning
- 1 teaspoon kosher salt
- Juice of ½ lime

- 8 large lettuce leaves
- 230 g prepared guacamole

Instructions:

1. Preheat the air fryer to 200°C.
2. In a large bowl, combine the chicken, onion, and peppers. Drizzle with the olive oil and toss until thoroughly coated. Add the fajita seasoning and salt and toss again.
3. Working in batches if necessary, arrange the chicken and vegetables in a single layer in the air fryer basket. Pausing halfway through the cooking time to shake the basket, air fry for 14 minutes, or until the vegetables are tender and a thermometer inserted into the thickest piece of chicken registers 76°C.
4. Transfer the mixture to a serving platter and drizzle with the fresh lime juice. Serve with the lettuce leaves and top with the guacamole.

Peanut Butter Chicken Satay

Serves 4

Prep time: 12 minutes / Cook time: 12 to 18 minutes

Ingredients:

- 120 g crunchy peanut butter
- 80 ml chicken broth
- 3 tablespoons low-sodium soy sauce
- 2 tablespoons freshly squeezed lemon juice
- 2 garlic cloves, minced
- 2 tablespoons extra-virgin olive oil
- 1 teaspoon curry powder
- 450 g chicken tenders
- Cooking oil spray

Instructions:

1. In a medium bowl, whisk the peanut butter, broth, soy sauce, lemon juice, garlic, olive oil, and curry powder until smooth.
2. Place 2 tablespoons of this mixture into a

small bowl. Transfer the remaining sauce to a serving bowl and set aside.

3. Add the chicken tenders to the bowl with the 2 tablespoons of sauce and stir to coat. Let stand for a few minutes to marinate.

4. Insert the crisper plate into the basket and the basket into the unit. Preheat the unit by selecting AIR FRY, setting the temperature to 200ºC, and setting the time to 3 minutes. Select START/STOP to begin.

5. Run a 6-inch bamboo skewer lengthwise through each chicken tender.

6. Once the unit is preheated, spray the crisper plate with cooking oil. Working in batches, place half the chicken skewers into the basket in a single layer without overlapping.

7. Select AIR FRY, set the temperature to 200ºC, and set the time to 9 minutes. Select START/STOP to begin.

8. After 6 minutes, check the chicken. If a food thermometer inserted into the chicken registers 76ºC, it is done. If not, resume cooking.

9. Repeat steps 6, 7, and 8 with the remaining chicken.

10. When the cooking is complete, serve the chicken with the reserved sauce.

Korean Honey Wings

Serves 4

Prep time: 10 minutes / Cook time: 25 minutes per batch

Ingredients:

- 55 g gochujang, or red pepper paste
- 55 g mayonnaise
- 2 tablespoons honey
- 1 tablespoon sesame oil
- 2 teaspoons minced garlic
- 1 tablespoon sugar
- 2 teaspoons ground ginger

Instructions:

1. 4 kg whole chicken wings
- Olive oil spray
- 1 teaspoon salt
- ½ teaspoon freshly ground black pepper

Instructions:

1. In a large bowl, whisk the gochujang, mayonnaise, honey, sesame oil, garlic, sugar, and ginger. Set aside.

2. Insert the crisper plate into the basket and the basket into the unit. Preheat the unit by selecting AIR FRY, setting the temperature to 200ºC, and setting the time to 3 minutes. Select START/STOP to begin.

3. To prepare the chicken wings, cut the wings in half. The meatier part is the drumette. Cut off and discard the wing tip from the flat part (or save the wing tips in the freezer to make chicken stock).

4. Once the unit is preheated, spray the crisper plate with olive oil. Working in batches, place half the chicken wings into the basket, spray them with olive oil, and sprinkle with the salt and pepper.

5. Select AIR FRY, set the temperature to 200ºC, and set the time to 20 minutes. Select START/STOP to begin.

6. After 10 minutes, remove the basket, flip the wings, and spray them with more olive oil. Reinsert the basket to resume cooking.

7. Cook the wings to an internal temperature of 76ºC, then transfer them to the bowl with the prepared sauce and toss to coat.

8. Repeat steps 4, 5, 6, and 7 for the remaining chicken wings.

9. Return the coated wings to the basket and air fry for 4 to 6 minutes more until the sauce has glazed the wings and the chicken is crisp. After 3 minutes, check the wings to make sure they aren't burning. Serve hot.

Chicken Enchiladas

Serves 4

Prep time: 10 minutes / Cook time: 8 minutes

Ingredients:

- Oil, for spraying
- 420 g shredded cooked chicken
- 1 package taco seasoning
- 8 flour tortillas, at room temperature
- 60 g canned black beans, rinsed and drained
- 1 (115 g) can diced green chilies, drained
- 1 (280 g) can red or green enchilada sauce
- 235 g shredded Cheddar cheese

Instructions:

1. Line the air fryer basket with parchment and spray lightly with oil. (Do not skip the step of lining the basket; the parchment will keep the sauce and cheese from dripping through the holes.)
2. In a small bowl, mix together the chicken and taco seasoning.
3. Divide the mixture among the tortillas. Top with the black beans and green chilis. Carefully roll up each tortilla.
4. Place the enchiladas, seam-side down, in the prepared basket. You may need to work in batches, depending on the size of your air fryer.
5. Spoon the enchilada sauce over the enchiladas. Use just enough sauce to keep them from drying out. You can add more sauce when serving. Sprinkle the cheese on top.
6. Air fry at 180°C for 5 to 8 minutes, or until heated through and the cheese is melted.
7. Place 2 enchiladas on each plate and top with more enchilada sauce, if desired.

Apricot-Glazed Turkey Tenderloin

Serves 4

Prep time: 20 minutes / Cook time: 30 minutes

Ingredients:

- Olive oil
- 80 g sugar-free apricot preserves
- ½ tablespoon spicy brown mustard
- 680 g turkey breast tenderloin
- Salt and freshly ground black pepper, to taste

Instructions:

1. Spray the air fryer basket lightly with olive oil.
2. In a small bowl, combine the apricot preserves and mustard to make a paste.
3. Season the turkey with salt and pepper. Spread the apricot paste all over the turkey.
4. Place the turkey in the air fryer basket and lightly spray with olive oil.
5. Air fry at 190°C for 15 minutes. Flip the turkey over and lightly spray with olive oil. Air fry until the internal temperature reaches at least 80°C, an additional 10 to 15 minutes.
6. Let the turkey rest for 10 minutes before slicing and serving.

Easy Turkey Tenderloin

Serves 4

Prep time: 20 minutes / Cook time: 30 minutes

Ingredients:

- Olive oil
- ½ teaspoon paprika
- ½ teaspoon garlic powder
- ½ teaspoon salt
- ½ teaspoon freshly ground black pepper
- Pinch cayenne pepper
- 680 g turkey breast tenderloin

Instructions:

1. Spray the air fryer basket lightly with olive oil.
2. In a small bowl, combine the paprika, garlic powder, salt, black pepper, and cayenne pepper. Rub the mixture all over the turkey.
3. Place the turkey in the air fryer basket and lightly spray with olive oil.
4. Air fry at 190°C for 15 minutes. Flip the turkey over and lightly spray with olive oil. Air fry until the internal temperature reaches at least 80°C for an additional 10 to 15 minutes.
5. Let the turkey rest for 10 minutes before slicing and serving.

Bacon-Wrapped Chicken Breasts Rolls

Serves 4

Prep time: 10 minutes / Cook time: 15 minutes

Ingredients:

- 15 g chopped fresh chives
- 2 tablespoons lemon juice
- 1 teaspoon dried sage
- 1 teaspoon fresh rosemary leaves
- 15 g fresh parsley leaves
- 4 cloves garlic, peeled
- 1 teaspoon ground fennel
- 3 teaspoons sea salt
- ½ teaspoon red pepper flakes
- 4 (115 g) boneless, skinless chicken breasts, pounded to ¼ inch thick
- 8 slices bacon
- Sprigs of fresh rosemary, for garnish
- Cooking spray

Instructions:

1. Preheat the air fryer to 170°C. Spritz the air fryer basket with cooking spray.
2. Put the chives, lemon juice, sage, rosemary, parsley, garlic, fennel, salt, and red pepper flakes in a food processor, then pulse to purée until smooth.
3. Unfold the chicken breasts on a clean work surface, then brush the top side of the chicken breasts with the sauce.
4. Roll the chicken breasts up from the shorter side, then wrap each chicken rolls with 2 bacon slices to cover. Secure with toothpicks.
5. Arrange the rolls in the preheated air fryer, then cook for 10 minutes. Flip the rolls halfway through.
6. Increase the heat to 200°C and air fry for 5 more minutes or until the bacon is browned and crispy.
7. Transfer the rolls to a large plate. Discard the toothpicks and spread with rosemary sprigs before serving.

Cranberry Curry Chicken

Serves 4

Prep time: 12 minutes / Cook time: 18 minutes

Ingredients:

- 3 (140 g) low-sodium boneless, skinless chicken breasts, cut into 1½-inch cubes
- 2 teaspoons olive oil
- 2 tablespoons cornflour
- 1 tablespoon curry powder
- 1 tart apple, chopped
- 120 ml low-sodium chicken broth
- 60 g dried cranberries
- 2 tablespoons freshly squeezed orange juice
- Brown rice, cooked (optional)

Instructions:

1. Preheat the air fryer to 196°C.
2. In a medium bowl, mix the chicken and olive oil. Sprinkle with the cornflour and curry powder. Toss to coat. Stir in the apple and

transfer to a metal pan. Bake in the air fryer for 8 minutes, stirring once during cooking.

3. Add the chicken broth, cranberries, and orange juice. Bake for about 10 minutes more, or until the sauce is slightly thickened and the chicken reaches an internal temperature of 76°C on a meat thermometer. Serve over hot cooked brown rice, if desired.

Potato-Crusted Chicken

Serves 4

Prep time: 15 minutes / Cook time: 22 to 25 minutes

Ingredients:

- 60 g buttermilk
- 1 large egg, beaten
- 180 g instant potato flakes
- 20 g grated Parmesan cheese
- 1 teaspoon salt
- ½ teaspoon freshly ground black pepper
- 2 whole boneless, skinless chicken breasts (about 450 g each), halved
- 1 to 2 tablespoons oil

Instructions:

1. In a shallow bowl, whisk the buttermilk and egg until blended. In another shallow bowl, stir together the potato flakes, cheese, salt, and pepper.
2. One at a time, dip the chicken pieces in the buttermilk mixture and the potato flake mixture, coating thoroughly.
3. Preheat the air fryer to 200°C. Line the air fryer basket with parchment paper.
4. Place the coated chicken on the parchment and spritz with oil.
5. Cook for 15 minutes. Flip the chicken, spritz it with oil, and cook for 7 to 10 minutes more until the outside is crispy and the inside is no longer pink.

Blackened Cajun Chicken Tenders

Serves 4

Prep time: 10 minutes / Cook time: 17 minutes

Ingredients:

- 2 teaspoons paprika
- 1 teaspoon chili powder
- ½ teaspoon garlic powder
- ½ teaspoon dried thyme
- ¼ teaspoon onion powder
- ⅛ teaspoon ground cayenne pepper
- 2 tablespoons coconut oil
- 450 g boneless, skinless chicken tenders
- 60 ml full-fat ranch dressing

Instructions:

1. In a small bowl, combine all seasonings.
2. Drizzle oil over chicken tenders and then generously coat each tender in the spice mixture. Place tenders into the air fryer basket.
3. Adjust the temperature to (190°C and air fry for 17 minutes.
4. Tenders will be 76°C internally when fully cooked. Serve with ranch dressing for dipping.

Coriander Chicken Kebabs

Serves 4

Prep time: 30 minutes / Cook time: 10 minutes

Ingredients:

- Chutney:
- 40 g unsweetened shredded coconut
- 120 ml hot water
- 40 g fresh coriander leaves, roughly chopped
- 10 g fresh mint leaves, roughly chopped
- 6 cloves garlic, roughly chopped
- 1 jalapeño, seeded and roughly chopped
- 60-75 ml water, as needed

- Juice of 1 lemon
- Chicken:
- 450 g boneless, skinless chicken thighs, cut crosswise into thirds
- Olive oil spray

Instructions:

1. For the chutney: In a blender or food processor, combine the coconut and hot water; set aside to soak for 5 minutes.
2. To the processor, add the coriander, mint, garlic, and jalapeño, along with 60 ml water. Blend at low speed, stopping occasionally to scrape down the sides. Add the lemon juice. With the blender or processor running, add only enough additional water to keep the contents moving. Turn the blender to high once the contents are moving freely and blend until the mixture is puréed.
3. For the chicken: Place the chicken pieces in a large bowl. Add ¼ cup of the chutney and mix well to coat. Set aside the remaining chutney to use as a dip. Marinate the chicken for 15 minutes at room temperature.
4. Spray the air fryer basket with olive oil spray. Arrange the chicken in the air fryer basket. Set the air fryer to 180ºC for 10 minutes. Use a meat thermometer to ensure that the chicken has reached an internal temperature of 76ºC.
5. Serve the chicken with the remaining chutney.

Turkish Chicken Kebabs

Serves 4

Prep time: 30 minutes / Cook time: 15 minutes

Ingredients:

- 70 g plain Greek yogurt
- 1 tablespoon minced garlic
- 1 tablespoon tomato paste
- 1 tablespoon fresh lemon juice
- 1 tablespoon vegetable oil
- 1 teaspoon kosher salt
- 1 teaspoon ground cumin
- 1 teaspoon sweet Hungarian paprika
- ½ teaspoon ground cinnamon
- ½ teaspoon black pepper
- ½ teaspoon cayenne pepper
- 450 g boneless, skinless chicken thighs, quartered crosswise

Instructions:

1. In a large bowl, combine the yogurt, garlic, tomato paste, lemon juice, vegetable oil, salt, cumin, paprika, cinnamon, black pepper, and cayenne. Stir until the spices are blended into the yogurt.
2. Add the chicken to the bowl and toss until well coated. Marinate at room temperature for 30 minutes, or cover and refrigerate for up to 24 hours.
3. Arrange the chicken in a single layer in the air fryer basket. Set the air fryer to (190ºC for 10 minutes. Turn the chicken and cook for 5 minutes more. Use a meat thermometer to ensure the chicken has reached an internal temperature of 76ºC.

Chicken Burgers with Ham and Cheese

Serves 4

Prep time: 12 minutes / Cook time: 13 to 16 minutes

Ingredients:

- 40 g soft bread crumbs
- 3 tablespoons milk
- 1 egg, beaten
- ½ teaspoon dried thyme
- Pinch salt
- Freshly ground black pepper, to taste
- 570 g chicken mince
- 70 g finely chopped ham

- 75 g grated Gouda cheese
- Olive oil for misting

Instructions:

1. Preheat the air fryer to 180°C.
2. In a medium bowl, combine the bread crumbs, milk, egg, thyme, salt, and pepper. Add the chicken and mix gently but thoroughly with clean hands.
3. Form the chicken into eight thin patties and place on waxed paper.
4. Top four of the patties with the ham and cheese. Top with remaining four patties and gently press the edges together to seal, so the ham and cheese mixture is in the middle of the burger.
5. Place the burgers in the basket and mist with olive oil. Bake for 13 to 16 minutes or until the chicken is thoroughly cooked to 76°C as measured with a meat thermometer. Serve immediately.

Thai Chicken with Cucumber and Chili Salad

Serves 6

Prep time: 25 minutes / Cook time: 25 minutes

Ingredients:

- 2 (570 g) small chickens, giblets discarded
- 1 tablespoon fish sauce
- 6 tablespoons chopped fresh coriander
- 2 teaspoons lime zest
- 1 teaspoon ground coriander
- 2 garlic cloves, minced
- 2 tablespoons packed light brown sugar
- 2 teaspoons vegetable oil
- Salt and ground black pepper, to taste
- 1 English cucumber, halved lengthwise and sliced thin
- 1 Thai chili, stemmed, deseeded, and minced
- 2 tablespoons chopped dry-roasted peanuts
- 1 small shallot, sliced thinly
- 1 tablespoon lime juice
- Lime wedges, for serving
- Cooking spray

Instructions:

1. Arrange a chicken on a clean work surface, remove the backbone with kitchen shears, then pound the chicken breast to flat. Cut the breast in half. Repeat with the remaining chicken.
2. Loose the breast and thigh skin with your fingers, then pat the chickens dry and pierce about 10 holes into the fat deposits of the chickens. Tuck the wings under the chickens.
3. Combine 2 teaspoons of fish sauce, coriander, lime zest, coriander, garlic, 4 teaspoons of sugar, 1 teaspoon of vegetable oil, ½ teaspoon of salt, and ⅛ teaspoon of ground black pepper in a small bowl. Stir to mix well.
4. Rub the fish sauce mixture under the breast and thigh skin of the game chickens, then let sit for 10 minutes to marinate.
5. Preheat the air fryer to 200°C. Spritz the air fryer basket with cooking spray.
6. Arrange the marinated chickens in the preheated air fryer, skin side down.
7. Air fry for 15 minutes, then gently turn the game hens over and air fry for 10 more minutes or until the skin is golden brown and the internal temperature of the chickens reads at least 76°C.
8. Meanwhile, combine all the remaining ingredients, except for the lime wedges, in a large bowl and sprinkle with salt and black pepper. Toss to mix well.
9. Transfer the fried chickens on a large plate, then sit the salad aside and squeeze the lime wedges over before serving.

Chapter 4 Fish and Seafood

Tuna Patty Sliders

Serves 4

Prep time: 15 minutes / Cook time: 10 to 15 minutes

Ingredients:

- 3 cans tuna, 140 g each, packed in water
- 40 g whole-wheat panko bread crumbs
- 50 g shredded Parmesan cheese
- 1 tablespoon Sriracha
- ¾ teaspoon black pepper
- 10 whole-wheat buns
- Cooking spray

Instructions:

1. Preheat the air fryer to 176ºC.
2. Spray the air fryer basket lightly with cooking spray.
3. In a medium bowl combine the tuna, bread crumbs, Parmesan cheese, Sriracha, and black pepper and stir to combine.
4. Form the mixture into 10 patties.
5. Place the patties in the air fryer basket in a single layer. Spray the patties lightly with cooking spray. You may need to cook them in batches.
6. Air fry for 6 to 8 minutes. Turn the patties over and lightly spray with cooking spray. Air fry until golden brown and crisp, another 4 to 7 more minutes. Serve warm.

Prawns Scampi

Serves 4

Prep time: 8 minutes / Cook time: 8 minutes

Ingredients:

- 4 tablespoons salted butter or ghee
- 1 tablespoon fresh lemon juice
- 1 tablespoon minced garlic
- 2 teaspoons red pepper flakes
- 455 g prawns (21 to 25 count), peeled and deveined
- 2 tablespoons dry white wine or chicken broth
- 2 tablespoons chopped fresh basil, plus more for sprinkling, or 1 teaspoon dried
- 1 tablespoon chopped fresh chives, or 1 teaspoon dried

Instructions:

1. Place a baking pan in the air fryer basket. Set the air fryer to 164ºC for 8 minutes (this will preheat the pan so the butter will melt faster).
2. Carefully remove the pan from the fryer and add the butter, lemon juice, garlic, and red pepper flakes. Place the pan back in the fryer.
3. Cook for 2 minutes, stirring once, until the butter has melted. (Do not skip this step; this is what infuses the butter with garlic flavor, which is what makes it all taste so good.)
4. Carefully remove the pan from the fryer and add the prawns, broth, basil, and chives. Stir gently until the ingredients are well combined.
5. Return the pan to the air fryer and cook for 5 minutes, stirring once.
6. Thoroughly stir the prawn mixture and let it rest for 1 minute on a wire rack. (This is so the prawns cook in the residual heat rather than getting overcooked and rubbery.)
7. Stir once more, sprinkle with additional chopped fresh basil, and serve.

Lemony Prawns and Courgette

Serves 4

Prep time: 15 minutes / Cook time: 7 to 8 minutes

Ingredients:

- 570 g extra-large raw prawns, peeled and deveined
- 2 medium courgettes (about 230 g each), halved lengthwise and cut into ½-inch-thick slices
- 1½ tablespoons olive oil
- ½ teaspoon garlic salt
- 1½ teaspoons dried oregano
- ⅛ teaspoon crushed red pepper flakes (optional)
- Juice of ½ lemon
- 1 tablespoon chopped fresh mint
- 1 tablespoon chopped fresh dill

Instructions:

1. Preheat the air fryer to 176°C.
2. In a large bowl, combine the prawns, courgette, oil, garlic salt, oregano, and pepper flakes (if using) and toss to coat.
3. Working in batches, arrange a single layer of the prawns and courgette in the air fryer basket. Air fry for 7 to 8 minutes, shaking the basket halfway, until the courgette is golden and the prawns are cooked through.
4. Transfer to a serving dish and tent with foil while you air fry the remaining prawns and courgette.
5. Top with the lemon juice, mint, and dill and serve.

Cajun and Lemon Pepper Cod

Makes 2 cod fillets

Prep time: 5 minutes / Cook time: 12 minutes

Ingredients:

- 1 tablespoon Cajun seasoning
- 1 teaspoon salt
- ½ teaspoon lemon pepper
- ½ teaspoon freshly ground black pepper
- 2 cod fillets, 230 g each, cut to fit into the air fryer basket
- Cooking spray
- 2 tablespoons unsalted butter, melted
- 1 lemon, cut into 4 wedges

Instructions:

1. Preheat the air fryer to 182°C. Spritz the air fryer basket with cooking spray.
2. Thoroughly combine the Cajun seasoning, salt, lemon pepper, and black pepper in a small bowl. Rub this mixture all over the cod fillets until completely coated.
3. Put the fillets in the air fryer basket and brush the melted butter over both sides of each fillet.
4. Bake in the preheated air fryer for 12 minutes, flipping the fillets halfway through, or until the fish flakes easily with a fork.
5. Remove the fillets from the basket and serve with fresh lemon wedges.

Classic Prawns Empanadas

Serves 5

Prep time: 10 minutes / Cook time: 8 minutes

Ingredients:

- 230 g raw prawns, peeled, deveined and chopped
- 1 small chopped red onion
- 1 spring onion, chopped
- 2 garlic cloves, minced
- 2 tablespoons minced red bell pepper
- 2 tablespoons chopped fresh coriander
- ½ tablespoon fresh lime juice
- ¼ teaspoon sweet paprika
- ⅛ teaspoon kosher salt
- ⅛ teaspoon crushed red pepper flakes

(optional)

- 1 large egg, beaten
- 10 frozen Goya Empanada Discos, thawed
- Cooking spray

Instructions:

1. In a medium bowl, combine the prawns, red onion, spring onion, garlic, bell pepper, coriander, lime juice, paprika, salt, and pepper flakes (if using).
2. In a small bowl, beat the egg with 1 teaspoon water until smooth.
3. Place an empanada disc on a work surface and put 2 tablespoons of the prawn mixture in the center. Brush the outer edges of the disc with the egg wash. Fold the disc over and gently press the edges to seal. Use a fork and press around the edges to crimp and seal completely. Brush the tops of the empanadas with the egg wash.
4. Preheat the air fryer to 192°C.
5. Spray the bottom of the air fryer basket with cooking spray to prevent sticking. Working in batches, arrange a single layer of the empanadas in the air fryer basket and air fry for about 8 minutes, flipping halfway, until golden brown and crispy.
6. Serve hot.

Air Fried Crab Bun

Serves 2

Prep time: 15 minutes / Cook time: 20 minutes

Ingredients:

- 140 g crab meat, chopped
- 2 eggs, beaten
- 2 tablespoons coconut flour
- ¼ teaspoon baking powder
- ½ teaspoon coconut aminos, or tamari
- ½ teaspoon ground black pepper
- 1 tablespoon coconut oil, softened

Instructions:

1. In the mixing bowl, mix crab meat with eggs, coconut flour, baking powder, coconut aminos, ground black pepper, and coconut oil.
2. Knead the smooth dough and cut it into pieces.
3. Make the buns from the crab mixture and put them in the air fryer basket.
4. Cook the crab buns at 185°C for 20 minutes.

Roasted Cod with Lemon-Garlic Potatoes

Serves 2

Prep time: 10 minutes / Cook time: 28 minutes

Ingredients:

- 3 tablespoons unsalted butter, softened, divided
- 2 garlic cloves, minced
- 1 lemon, grated to yield 2 teaspoons zest and sliced ¼ inch thick
- Salt and pepper, to taste
- 1 large russet potato (about 340 g), unpeeled, sliced ¼ inch thick
- 1 tablespoon minced fresh parsley, chives, or tarragon
- 2 (230 g) skinless cod fillets, 1¼ inches thick
- Vegetable oil spray

Instructions:

1. Preheat the air fryer to 204°C.
2. Make foil sling for air fryer basket by folding 1 long sheet of aluminum foil so it is 4 inches wide. Lay sheet of foil widthwise across basket, pressing foil into and up sides of basket. Fold excess foil as needed so that edges of foil are flush with top of basket. Lightly spray the foil and basket with vegetable oil spray.
3. Microwave 1 tablespoon butter, garlic, 1 teaspoon lemon zest, ¼ teaspoon salt, and ⅛

teaspoon pepper in a medium bowl, stirring once, until the butter is melted and the mixture is fragrant, about 30 seconds. Add the potato slices and toss to coat. Shingle the potato slices on sling in prepared basket to create 2 even layers. Air fry until potato slices are spotty brown and just tender, 16 to 18 minutes, using a sling to rotate potatoes halfway through cooking.

4. Combine the remaining 2 tablespoons butter, remaining 1 teaspoon lemon zest, and parsley in a small bowl. Pat the cod dry with paper towels and season with salt and pepper. Place the fillets, skinned-side down, on top of potato slices, spaced evenly apart. (Tuck thinner tail ends of fillets under themselves as needed to create uniform pieces.) Dot the fillets with the butter mixture and top with the lemon slices. Return the basket to the air fryer and air fry until the cod flakes apart when gently prodded with a paring knife and registers 60°C, 12 to 15 minutes, using a sling to rotate the potato slices and cod halfway through cooking.

5. Using a sling, carefully remove potatoes and cod from air fryer. Cut the potato slices into 2 portions between fillets using fish spatula. Slide spatula along underside of potato slices and transfer with cod to individual plates. Serve.

Seasoned Tuna Steaks

Serves 4

Prep time: 5 minutes / Cook time: 9 minutes

Ingredients:

- 1 teaspoon garlic powder
- ½ teaspoon salt
- ¼ teaspoon dried thyme
- ¼ teaspoon dried oregano
- 4 tuna steaks
- 2 tablespoons olive oil
- 1 lemon, quartered

Instructions:

1. Preheat the air fryer to 192°C.
2. In a small bowl, whisk together the garlic powder, salt, thyme, and oregano.
3. Coat the tuna steaks with olive oil. Season both sides of each steak with the seasoning blend. Place the steaks in a single layer in the air fryer basket.
4. Roast for 5 minutes, then flip and roast for an additional 3 to 4 minutes.

Garlic Prawns

Serves 3

Prep time: 15 minutes / Cook time: 10 minutes

Ingredients:

Prawns:

- Olive or vegetable oil, for spraying
- 450 g medium raw prawns, peeled and deveined
- 6 tablespoons unsalted butter, melted
- 120 g panko bread crumbs
- 2 tablespoons garlic granules
- 1 teaspoon salt
- ½ teaspoon freshly ground black pepper

Garlic Butter Sauce:

- 115 g unsalted butter
- 2 teaspoons garlic granules
- ¾ teaspoon salt (omit if using salted butter)

Make the Prawns Instructions:

1. Preheat the air fryer to 204°C. Line the air fryer basket with baking paper and spray lightly with oil.
2. Place the prawns and melted butter in a zip-top plastic bag, seal, and shake well, until evenly coated.
3. In a medium bowl, mix together the breadcrumbs,

garlic, salt, and black pepper.

4. Add the prawns to the panko mixture and toss until evenly coated. Shake off any excess coating.

5. Place the prawns in the prepared basket and spray lightly with oil.

6. Cook for 8 to 10 minutes, flipping and spraying with oil after 4 to 5 minutes, until golden brown and crispy. Make the Garlic Butter Sauce

7. In a microwave-safe bowl, combine the butter, garlic, and salt and microwave on 50% power for 30 to 60 seconds, stirring every 15 seconds, until completely melted.

8. Serve the prawns immediately with the garlic butter sauce on the side for dipping.

Tuna and Fruit Kebabs

Serves 4

Prep time: 15 minutes / Cook time: 8 to 12 minutes

Ingredients:

- 455 g tuna steaks, cut into 1-inch cubes
- 85 g canned pineapple chunks, drained, juice reserved
- 75 g large red grapes
- 1 tablespoon honey
- 2 teaspoons grated fresh ginger
- 1 teaspoon olive oil
- Pinch cayenne pepper

Instructions:

1. Thread the tuna, pineapple, and grapes on 8 bamboo or 4 metal skewers that fit in the air fryer.

2. In a small bowl, whisk the honey, 1 tablespoon of reserved pineapple juice, the ginger, olive oil, and cayenne. Brush this mixture over the kebabs. Let them stand for 10 minutes.

3. Air fry the kebabs at 188ºC for 8 to 12 minutes, or until the tuna reaches an internal temperature

of at least 64ºC on a meat thermometer, and the fruit is tender and glazed, brushing once with the remaining sauce. Discard any remaining marinade. Serve immediately.

BBQ Prawns with Creole Butter Sauce

Serves 4

Prep time: 10 minutes / Cook time: 12 to 15 minutes

Ingredients:

- 6 tablespoons unsalted butter
- 80 ml Worcestershire sauce
- 3 cloves garlic, minced
- Juice of 1 lemon
- 1 teaspoon paprika
- 1 teaspoon Creole seasoning
- 680 g large uncooked prawns, peeled and deveined
- 2 tablespoons fresh parsley

Instructions:

1. Preheat the air fryer to 188ºC.

2. In a large microwave-safe bowl, combine the butter, Worcestershire, and garlic. Microwave on high for 1 to 2 minutes until the butter is melted. Stir in the lemon juice, paprika, and Creole seasoning. Add the prawns and toss until thoroughly coated.

3. Transfer the mixture to a casserole dish or pan that fits in your air fryer. Pausing halfway through the cooking time to turn the prawns, air fry for 12 to 15 minutes, until the prawns are cooked through. Top with the parsley just before serving.

Firecracker Prawns

Serves 4

Prep time: 10 minutes / Cook time: 7 minutes

Ingredients:

- 455 g medium prawns, peeled and deveined
- 2 tablespoons salted butter, melted
- ½ teaspoon Old Bay seasoning
- ¼ teaspoon garlic powder
- 2 tablespoons Sriracha
- ¼ teaspoon powdered sweetener
- 60 ml full-fat mayonnaise
- ⅛ teaspoon ground black pepper

Instructions:

1. In a large bowl, toss prawns in butter, Old Bay seasoning, and garlic powder. Place prawns into the air fryer basket.
2. Adjust the temperature to 204ºC and set the timer for 7 minutes.
3. Flip the prawns halfway through the cooking time. Prawns will be bright pink when fully cooked.
4. In another large bowl, mix Sriracha, sweetener, mayonnaise, and pepper. Toss prawns in the spicy mixture and serve immediately.

Snapper with Shallot and Tomato

Serves 2

Prep time: 20 minutes / Cook time: 15 minutes

Ingredients:

- 2 snapper fillets
- 1 shallot, peeled and sliced
- 2 garlic cloves, halved
- 1 bell pepper, sliced
- 1 small-sized serrano pepper, sliced
- 1 tomato, sliced
- 1 tablespoon olive oil
- ¼ teaspoon freshly ground black pepper
- ½ teaspoon paprika
- Sea salt, to taste
- 2 bay leaves

Instructions:

1. Place two baking paper sheets on a working surface. Place the fish in the center of one side of the baking paper.
2. Top with the shallot, garlic, peppers, and tomato. Drizzle olive oil over the fish and vegetables. Season with black pepper, paprika, and salt. Add the bay leaves.
3. Fold over the other half of the baking paper. Now, fold the paper around the edges tightly and create a half moon shape, sealing the fish inside.
4. Cook in the preheated air fryer at 200ºC for 15 minutes. Serve warm.

Sea Bass with Avocado Cream

Serves 4

Prep time: 30 minutes / Cook time: 9 minutes

Ingredients:

- Fish Fillets:
- 1½ tablespoons balsamic vinegar
- 120 ml vegetable broth
- ⅓ teaspoon shallot powder
- 1 tablespoon coconut aminos, or tamari
- 4 Sea Bass fillets
- 1 teaspoon ground black pepper
- 1½ tablespoons olive oil
- Fine sea salt, to taste
- ⅓ teaspoon garlic powder
- Avocado Cream:
- 2 tablespoons Greek-style yogurt
- 1 clove garlic, peeled and minced
- 1 teaspoon ground black pepper
- ½ tablespoon olive oil
- 80 ml vegetable broth
- 1 avocado
- ½ teaspoon lime juice
- ⅓ teaspoon fine sea salt

Instructions:

1. In a bowl, wash and pat the fillets dry using some paper towels. Add all the seasonings. In another bowl, stir in the remaining ingredients for the fish fillets.
2. Add the seasoned fish fillets; cover and let the fillets marinate in your refrigerator at least 3 hours.
3. Then, set the air fryer to 164°C. Cook marinated sea bass fillets in the air fryer grill basket for 9 minutes.
4. In the meantime, prepare the avocado sauce by mixing all the ingredients with an immersion blender or regular blender. Serve the sea bass fillets topped with the avocado sauce. Enjoy!

Tex-Mex Salmon Bowl

Serves 4

Prep time: 15 minutes / Cook time: 9 to 14 minutes

Ingredients:

- 340 g salmon fillets, cut into 1½-inch cubes
- 1 red onion, chopped
- 1 jalapeño pepper, minced
- 1 red bell pepper, chopped
- 60 ml salsa
- 2 teaspoons peanut or safflower oil
- 2 tablespoons tomato juice
- 1 teaspoon chilli powder

Instructions:

1. Preheat the air fryer to 188°C.
2. Mix together the salmon cubes, red onion, jalapeño, red bell pepper, salsa, peanut oil, tomato juice, chilli powder in a medium metal bowl and stir until well incorporated.
3. Transfer the bowl to the air fryer basket and bake for 9 to 14 minutes, stirring once, or until the salmon is cooked through and the veggies are fork-tender.

4. Serve warm.

Panko-Crusted Fish Sticks

Serves 4

Prep time: 10 minutes / Cook time: 15 minutes

Ingredients:

Tartar Sauce:
- 470 ml mayonnaise
- 2 tablespoons dill pickle relish
- 1 tablespoon dried minced onions

Fish Sticks:
- Olive or vegetable oil, for spraying
- 455 g tilapia fillets
- 75 g plain flour
- 120 g panko bread crumbs
- 2 tablespoons Creole seasoning
- 2 teaspoons garlic granules
- 1 teaspoon onion powder
- ½ teaspoon salt
- ¼ teaspoon freshly ground black pepper
- 1 large egg

Make the Tartar Sauce: Instructions:

1. In a small bowl, whisk together the mayonnaise, pickle relish, and onions. Cover with plastic wrap and refrigerate until ready to serve. You can make this sauce ahead of time; the flavors will intensify as it chills. Make the Fish Sticks:
2. Preheat the air fryer to 176°C. Line the air fryer basket with baking paper and spray lightly with oil.
3. Cut the fillets into equal-size sticks and place them in a zip-top plastic bag.
4. Add the flour to the bag, seal, and shake well until evenly coated.
5. In a shallow bowl, mix together the bread crumbs, Creole seasoning, garlic, onion powder, salt, and black pepper.
6. In a small bowl, whisk the egg.

7. Dip the fish sticks in the egg, then dredge in the bread crumb mixture until completely coated.
8. Place the fish sticks in the prepared basket. You may need to work in batches, depending on the size of your air fryer. Do not overcrowd. Spray lightly with oil.
9. Cook for 12 to 15 minutes, or until browned and cooked through. Serve with the tartar sauce.

Black Cod with Grapes and Kale

Serves 2

Prep time: 10 minutes / Cook time: 15 minutes

Ingredients:

- 2 fillets of black cod, 200 g each
- Salt and freshly ground black pepper, to taste
- Olive oil
- 150 g grapes, halved
- 1 small bulb fennel, sliced ¼-inch thick
- 65 g pecans
- 200 g shredded kale
- 2 teaspoons white balsamic vinegar or white wine vinegar
- 2 tablespoons extra-virgin olive oil

Instructions:

1. Preheat the air fryer to 204°C.
2. Season the cod fillets with salt and pepper and drizzle, brush or spray a little olive oil on top. Place the fish, presentation side up (skin side down), into the air fryer basket. Air fry for 10 minutes.
3. When the fish has finished cooking, remove the fillets to a side plate and loosely tent with foil to rest.
4. Toss the grapes, fennel and pecans in a bowl with a drizzle of olive oil and season with salt and pepper. Add the grapes, fennel and pecans to the air fryer basket and air fry for 5 minutes, shaking the basket once during the cooking time.
5. Transfer the grapes, fennel and pecans to a bowl with the kale. Dress the kale with the balsamic vinegar and olive oil, season to taste with salt and pepper and serve alongside the cooked fish.

Garlic Lemon Scallops

Serves 4

Prep time: 5 minutes / Cook time: 10 minutes

Ingredients:

- 4 tablespoons salted butter, melted
- 4 teaspoons peeled and finely minced garlic
- ½ small lemon, zested and juiced
- 8 sea scallops, 30 g each, cleaned and patted dry
- ¼ teaspoon salt
- ¼ teaspoon ground black pepper

Instructions:

1. In a small bowl, mix butter, garlic, lemon zest, and lemon juice. Place scallops in an ungreased round nonstick baking dish. Pour butter mixture over scallops, then sprinkle with salt and pepper.
2. Place dish into air fryer basket. Adjust the temperature to 182°C and bake for 10 minutes. Scallops will be opaque and firm, and have an internal temperature of 56°C when done. Serve warm.

Mediterranean-Style Cod

Serves 4

Prep time: 5 minutes / Cook time: 12 minutes

Ingredients:

- 4 cod fillets, 170 g each
- 3 tablespoons fresh lemon juice
- 1 tablespoon olive oil

- ¼ teaspoon salt
- 6 cherry tomatoes, halved
- 45 g pitted and sliced kalamata olives

Instructions:

1. Place cod into an ungreased round nonstick baking dish. Pour lemon juice into dish and drizzle cod with olive oil. Sprinkle with salt. Place tomatoes and olives around baking dish in between fillets.
2. Place dish into air fryer basket. Adjust the temperature to 176°C and bake for 12 minutes, carefully turning cod halfway through cooking. Fillets will be lightly browned, easily flake, and have an internal temperature of at least 64°C when done. Serve warm.

Rainbow Salmon Kebabs

Serves 2

Prep time: 10 minutes / Cook time: 8 minutes

Ingredients:

- 170 g boneless, skinless salmon, cut into 1-inch cubes
- ¼ medium red onion, peeled and cut into 1-inch pieces
- ½ medium yellow bell pepper, seeded and cut into 1-inch pieces
- ½ medium courgette, trimmed and cut into ½-inch slices
- 1 tablespoon olive oil
- ½ teaspoon salt
- ¼ teaspoon ground black pepper

Instructions:

1. Using one (6-inch) skewer, skewer 1 piece salmon, then 1 piece onion, 1 piece bell pepper, and finally 1 piece courgette. Repeat this pattern with additional skewers to make four kebabs total. Drizzle with olive oil and

sprinkle with salt and black pepper.
2. Place kebabs into ungreased air fryer basket. Adjust the temperature to 204°C and air fry for 8 minutes, turning kebabs halfway through cooking. Salmon will easily flake and have an internal temperature of at least 64°C when done; vegetables will be tender. Serve warm.

Confetti Salmon Burgers

Serves 4

Prep time: 10 minutes / Cook time: 12 minutes

Ingredients:

- 400 g cooked fresh or canned salmon, flaked with a fork
- 40 g minced spring onions, white and light green parts only
- 40 g minced red bell pepper
- 40 g minced celery
- 2 small lemons
- 1 teaspoon crab boil seasoning such as Old Bay
- ½ teaspoon kosher or coarse sea salt
- ½ teaspoon black pepper
- 1 egg, beaten
- 30 g fresh bread crumbs
- Vegetable oil, for spraying

Instructions:

1. In a large bowl, combine the salmon, vegetables, the zest and juice of 1 of the lemons, crab boil seasoning, salt, and pepper. Add the egg and bread crumbs and stir to combine. Form the mixture into 4 patties weighing approximately 140 g each. Chill until firm, about 15 minutes.
2. Preheat the air fryer to 204°C.
3. Spray the salmon patties with oil on all sides and spray the air fryer basket to prevent sticking. Air fry for 12 minutes, flipping

halfway through, until the burgers are browned and cooked through. Cut the remaining lemon into 4 wedges and serve with the burgers.

Fish Fillets with Lemon-Dill Sauce

Serves 4

Prep time: 5 minutes / Cook time: 7 minutes

Ingredients:

- 455 g snapper, grouper, or salmon fillets
- Sea salt and freshly ground black pepper, to taste
- 1 tablespoon avocado oil
- 60 g sour cream
- 60 g mayonnaise
- 2 tablespoons fresh dill, chopped, plus more for garnish
- 1 tablespoon freshly squeezed lemon juice
- ½ teaspoon grated lemon zest

Instructions:

1. Pat the fish dry with paper towels and season well with salt and pepper. Brush with the avocado oil.
2. Set the air fryer to 204°C. Place the fillets in the air fryer basket and air fry for 1 minute.
3. Lower the air fryer temperature to 164°C and continue cooking for 5 minutes. Flip the fish and cook for 1 minute more or until an instant-read thermometer reads 64°C. (If using salmon, cook it to 52°C /125°F for medium-rare.)
4. While the fish is cooking, make the sauce by combining the sour cream, mayonnaise, dill, lemon juice, and lemon zest in a medium bowl. Season with salt and pepper and stir until combined. Refrigerate until ready to serve.
5. Serve the fish with the sauce, garnished with

the remaining dill.

Lemon Mahi-Mahi

Serves 2

Prep time: 5 minutes / Cook time: 14 minutes

Ingredients:

- Olive or vegetable oil, for spraying
- 2 (170 g) mahi-mahi fillets
- 1 tablespoon lemon juice
- 1 tablespoon olive oil
- ¼ teaspoon salt
- ¼ teaspoon freshly ground black pepper
- 1 tablespoon chopped fresh dill
- 2 lemon slices

Instructions:

1. Line the air fryer basket with baking paper and spray lightly with oil.
2. Place the mahi-mahi in the prepared basket.
3. In a small bowl, whisk together the lemon juice and olive oil. Brush the mixture evenly over the mahi-mahi.
4. Sprinkle the mahi-mahi with the salt and black pepper and top with the dill.
5. Air fry at 204°C for 12 to 14 minutes, depending on the thickness of the fillets, until they flake easily.
6. Transfer to plates, top each with a lemon slice, and serve.

Prawn Kebabs

Serves 4

Prep time: 15 minutes / Cook time: 6 minutes

Ingredients:

- Olive or vegetable oil, for spraying
- 455 g medium raw prawns, peeled and deveined
- 4 tablespoons unsalted butter, melted

- 1 tablespoon Old Bay seasoning
- 1 tablespoon packed light brown sugar
- 1 teaspoon granulated garlic
- 1 teaspoon onion powder
- ½ teaspoon freshly ground black pepper

Instructions:

1. Line the air fryer basket with baking paper and spray lightly with oil.
2. Thread the prawns onto the skewers and place them in the prepared basket.
3. In a small bowl, mix together the butter, Old Bay, brown sugar, garlic, onion powder, and black pepper. Brush the sauce on the prawns.
4. Air fry at 204ºC for 5 to 6 minutes, or until pink and firm. Serve immediately.

Breaded Prawns Tacos

Makes 8 tacos

Prep time: 10 minutes / Cook time: 9 minutes

Ingredients:

- 2 large eggs
- 1 teaspoon prepared yellow mustard
- 455 g small prawns, peeled, deveined, and tails removed
- 45 g finely shredded Gouda or Parmesan cheese
- 80 g pork scratchings ground to dust

For Serving:

- 8 large round lettuce leaves
- 60 ml pico de gallo
- 20 g shredded purple cabbage
- 1 lemon, sliced
- Guacamole (optional)

Instructions:

1. Preheat the air fryer to 204ºC.
2. Crack the eggs into a large bowl, add the mustard, and whisk until well combined. Add the prawns and stir well to coat.
3. In a medium-sized bowl, mix together the cheese and pork scratching dust until well combined.
4. One at a time, roll the coated prawns in the pork scratching dust mixture and use your hands to press it onto each prawns. Spray the coated prawns with avocado oil and place them in the air fryer basket, leaving space between them.
5. Air fry the prawns for 9 minutes, or until cooked through and no longer translucent, flipping after 4 minutes.
6. To serve, place a lettuce leaf on a serving plate, place several prawns on top, and top with 1½ teaspoons each of pico de gallo and purple cabbage. Squeeze some lemon juice on top and serve with guacamole, if desired.
7. Store leftover prawns in an airtight container in the refrigerator for up to 3 days. Reheat in a preheated 204ºC air fryer for 5 minutes, or until warmed through.

Chapter 5 Beef, Pork, and Lamb

Mexican-Style Shredded Beef

Serves 6

Prep time: 5 minutes / Cook time: 35 minutes

Ingredients:
- 1 (900 g) beef braising steak, cut into 2-inch cubes
- 1 teaspoon salt
- ½ teaspoon ground black pepper
- 120 ml no-sugar-added chipotle sauce

Instructions:
1. In a large bowl, sprinkle beef cubes with salt and pepper and toss to coat. Place beef into ungreased air fryer basket. Adjust the temperature to 204°C and air fry for 30 minutes, shaking the basket halfway through cooking. Beef will be done when internal temperature is at least 72°C.
2. Place cooked beef into a large bowl and shred with two forks. Pour in chipotle sauce and toss to coat.
3. Return beef to air fryer basket for an additional 5 minutes at 204°C to crisp with sauce. Serve warm.

Mustard Herb Pork Tenderloin

Serves 6

Prep time: 5 minutes / Cook time: 20 minutes

Ingredients:
- 60 ml mayonnaise
- 2 tablespoons Dijon mustard
- ½ teaspoon dried thyme
- ¼ teaspoon dried rosemary
- 1 (450 g) pork tenderloin
- ½ teaspoon salt
- ¼ teaspoon ground black pepper

Instructions:
1. In a small bowl, mix mayonnaise, mustard, thyme, and rosemary. Brush tenderloin with mixture on all sides, then sprinkle with salt and pepper on all sides.
2. Place tenderloin into ungreased air fryer basket. Adjust the temperature to 204°C and air fry for 20 minutes, turning tenderloin halfway through cooking. Tenderloin will be golden and have an internal temperature of at least 64°C when done. Serve warm.

Spice-Rubbed Pork Loin

Serves 6

Prep time: 5 minutes / Cook time: 20 minutes

Ingredients:
- 1 teaspoon paprika
- ½ teaspoon ground cumin
- ½ teaspoon chili powder
- ½ teaspoon garlic powder
- 2 tablespoons coconut oil
- 1 (680 g) boneless pork loin
- ½ teaspoon salt
- ¼ teaspoon ground black pepper

Instructions:
1. In a small bowl, mix paprika, cumin, chili powder, and garlic powder.
2. Drizzle coconut oil over pork. Sprinkle pork loin with salt and pepper, then rub spice mixture evenly on all sides.
3. Place pork loin into ungreased air fryer basket. Adjust the temperature to 204°C and air fry for 20 minutes, turning pork halfway through cooking. Pork loin will be browned and have an internal temperature of at least 64°C when done. Serve warm.

Buttery Pork Chops

Serves 4

Prep time: 5 minutes / Cook time: 12 minutes

Ingredients:

- 4 (110 g) boneless pork chops
- ½ teaspoon salt
- ¼ teaspoon ground black pepper
- 2 tablespoons salted butter, softened

Instructions:

1. Sprinkle pork chops on all sides with salt and pepper. Place chops into ungreased air fryer basket in a single layer. Adjust the temperature to 204°C and air fry for 12 minutes. Pork chops will be golden and have an internal temperature of at least 64°C when done.
2. Use tongs to remove cooked pork chops from air fryer and place onto a large plate. Top each chop with ½ tablespoon butter and let sit 2 minutes to melt. Serve warm.

Honey-Baked Pork Loin

Serves 6

Prep time: 30 minutes / Cook time: 22 to 25 minutes

Ingredients:

- 60 ml honey
- 60 ml freshly squeezed lemon juice
- 2 tablespoons soy sauce
- 1 teaspoon garlic powder
- 1 (900 g) pork loin
- 2 tablespoons vegetable oil

Instructions:

1. In a medium bowl, whisk together the honey, lemon juice, soy sauce, and garlic powder. Reserve half of the mixture for basting during cooking.
2. Cut 5 slits in the pork loin and transfer it to a resealable bag. Add the remaining honey mixture. Seal the bag and refrigerate to marinate for at least 2 hours.
3. Preheat the air fryer to 204°C. Line the air fryer basket with parchment paper.
4. Remove the pork from the marinade, and place it on the parchment. Spritz with oil, then baste with the reserved marinade.
5. Cook for 15 minutes. Flip the pork, baste with more marinade and spritz with oil again. Cook for 7 to 10 minutes more until the internal temperature reaches 64°C. Let rest for 5 minutes before serving.

Greek Lamb Rack

Serves 4

Prep time: 5 minutes / Cook time: 10 minutes

Ingredients:

- 60 ml freshly squeezed lemon juice
- 1 teaspoon oregano
- 2 teaspoons minced fresh rosemary
- 1 teaspoon minced fresh thyme
- 2 tablespoons minced garlic
- Salt and freshly ground black pepper, to taste
- 2 to 4 tablespoons olive oil
- 1 lamb rib rack (7 to 8 ribs)

Instructions:

1. Preheat the air fryer to 182°C.
2. In a small mixing bowl, combine the lemon juice, oregano, rosemary, thyme, garlic, salt, pepper, and olive oil and mix well.
3. Rub the mixture over the lamb, covering all the meat. Put the rack of lamb in the air fryer. Roast for 10 minutes. Flip the rack halfway through.
4. After 10 minutes, measure the internal temperature of the rack of lamb reaches at least 64°C.
5. Serve immediately.

Bacon and Cheese Stuffed Pork Chops

Serves 4

Prep time: 10 minutes / Cook time: 12 minutes

Ingredients:

- 15 g plain pork scratchings, finely crushed
- 120 ml shredded sharp Cheddar cheese
- 4 slices cooked bacon, crumbled
- 4 (110 g) boneless pork chops
- ½ teaspoon salt
- ¼ teaspoon ground black pepper

Instructions:

1. In a small bowl, mix pork scratchings, Cheddar, and bacon.
2. Make a 3-inch slit in the side of each pork chop and stuff with ¼ pork rind mixture. Sprinkle each side of pork chops with salt and pepper.
3. Place pork chops into ungreased air fryer basket, stuffed side up. Adjust the temperature to 204ºC and air fry for 12 minutes. Pork chops will be browned and have an internal temperature of at least 64ºC when done. Serve warm.

Beef Burger

Serves 4

Prep time: 20 minutes / Cook time: 12 minutes

Ingredients:

- 570 g lean beef mince
- 1 tablespoon soy sauce or tamari
- 1 teaspoon Dijon mustard
- 1/2 teaspoon smoked paprika
- 1 teaspoon shallot powder
- 1 clove garlic, minced
- ½ teaspoon cumin powder
- 60 ml spring onions, minced
- ⅓ teaspoon sea salt flakes
- ⅓ teaspoon freshly cracked mixed peppercorns
- 1 teaspoon celery salt
- 1 teaspoon dried parsley

Instructions:

1. Mix all of the above ingredients in a bowl; knead until everything is well incorporated.
2. Shape the mixture into four patties. Next, make a shallow dip in the center of each patty to prevent them puffing up during air frying.
3. Spritz the patties on all sides using nonstick cooking spray. Cook approximately 12 minutes at 182ºC.
4. Check for doneness, an instant-read thermometer should read 72ºC. Bon appétit!

Pork Schnitzel with Dill Sauce

Serves 4 to 6

Prep time: 5 minutes / Cook time: 24 minutes

Ingredients:

- 6 bonelesspork chops (about 680 g)
- 120 ml flour
- 1½ teaspoons salt
- Freshly ground black pepper, to taste
- 2 eggs
- 120 ml milk
- 355 ml toasted fine bread crumbs
- 1 teaspoon paprika
- 3 tablespoons butter, melted
- 2 tablespoons vegetable or olive oil
- lemon wedges
- Dill Sauce:
- 235 ml chicken stock
- 1½ tablespoons cornflour
- 80 ml sour cream
- 1½ tablespoons chopped fresh dill
- Salt and pepper, to taste

Instructions:

1. Trim the excess fat from the pork chops and pound each chop with a meat mallet between

two pieces of plastic wrap until they are ½-inch thick.

2. Set up a dredging station. Combine the flour, salt, and black pepper in a shallow dish. Whisk the eggs and milk together in a second shallow dish. Finally, combine the bread crumbs and paprika in a third shallow dish.

3. Dip each flattened pork chop in the flour. Shake off the excess flour and dip each chop into the egg mixture. Finally dip them into the bread crumbs and press the bread crumbs onto the meat firmly. Place each finished chop on a baking sheet until they are all coated.

4. Preheat the air fryer to 204ºC.

5. Combine the melted butter and the oil in a small bowl and lightly brush both sides of the coated pork chops. Do not brush the chops too heavily or the breading will not be as crispy.

6. Air fry one schnitzel at a time for 4 minutes, turning it over halfway through the cooking time. Hold the cooked schnitzels warm on a baking pan in a 76ºC oven while you finish air frying the rest.

7. While the schnitzels are cooking, whisk the chicken stock and cornflour together in a small saucepan over medium-high heat on the stovetop. Bring the mixture to a boil and simmer for 2 minutes. Remove the saucepan from heat and whisk in the sour cream. Add the chopped fresh dill and season with salt and pepper.

8. Transfer the pork schnitzel to a platter and serve with dill sauce and lemon wedges.

Meat and Rice Stuffed Peppers

Serves 4

Prep time: 20 minutes / Cook time: 18 minutes

Ingredients:
- 340 g lean beef mince
- 110 g lean pork mince
- 60 ml onion, minced
- 1 (425 g) can finely-chopped tomatoes
- 1 teaspoon Worcestershire sauce
- 1 teaspoon barbecue seasoning
- 1 teaspoon honey
- ½ teaspoon dried basil
- 120 ml cooked brown rice
- ½ teaspoon garlic powder
- ½ teaspoon oregano
- ½ teaspoon salt
- 2 small peppers, cut in half, stems removed, deseeded
- Cooking spray

Instructions:
1. Preheat the air fryer to 182ºC and spritz a baking pan with cooking spray.

2. Arrange the beef, pork, and onion in the baking pan and bake in the preheated air fryer for 8 minutes. Break the ground meat into chunks halfway through the cooking.

3. Meanwhile, combine the tomatoes, Worcestershire sauce, barbecue seasoning, honey, and basil in a saucepan. Stir to mix well.

4. Transfer the cooked meat mixture to a large bowl and add the cooked rice, garlic powder, oregano, salt, and 60 ml of the tomato mixture. Stir to mix well.

5. Stuff the pepper halves with the mixture, then arrange the pepper halves in the air fryer and air fry for 10 minutes or until the peppers are lightly charred.

6. Serve the stuffed peppers with the remaining tomato sauce on top.

Mojito Lamb Chops

Serves 2

Prep time: 30 minutes / Cook time: 5 minutes

Ingredients:
Marinade:
- 2 teaspoons grated lime zest

- 120 ml lime juice
- 60 ml avocado oil
- 60 ml chopped fresh mint leaves
- 4 cloves garlic, roughly chopped
- 2 teaspoons fine sea salt
- ½ teaspoon ground black pepper
- 4 (1-inch-thick) lamb chops
- Sprigs of fresh mint, for garnish (optional)
- Lime slices, for serving (optional)

Instructions:

1. Make the marinade: Place all the ingredients for the marinade in a food processor or blender and purée until mostly smooth with a few small chunks. Transfer half of the marinade to a shallow dish and set the other half aside for serving. Add the lamb to the shallow dish, cover, and place in the refrigerator to marinate for at least 2 hours or overnight.
2. Spray the air fryer basket with avocado oil. Preheat the air fryer to 200°C.
3. Remove the chops from the marinade and place them in the air fryer basket. Air fry for 5 minutes, or until the internal temperature reaches 64°C for medium doneness.
4. Allow the chops to rest for 10 minutes before serving with the rest of the marinade as a sauce. Garnish with fresh mint leaves and serve with lime slices, if desired. Best served fresh.

Pork Medallions with Endive Salad

Serves 4

Prep time: 25 minutes / Cook time: 7 minutes

Ingredients:

- 1 (230 g) pork tenderloin
- Salt and freshly ground black pepper, to taste
- 60 ml flour
- 2 eggs, lightly beaten
- 180 ml finely crushed crackers
- 1 teaspoon paprika
- 1 teaspoon mustard powder

- 1 teaspoon garlic powder
- 1 teaspoon dried thyme
- 1 teaspoon salt
- vegetable or rapeseed oil, in spray bottle

Vinaigrette:
- 60 ml white balsamic vinegar
- 2 tablespoons agave syrup (or honey or maple syrup)
- 1 tablespoon Dijon mustard
- juice of ½ lemon
- 2 tablespoons chopped chervil or flat-leaf parsley
- salt and freshly ground black pepper
- 120 ml extra-virgin olive oil

Endive Salad:
- 1 heart romaine lettuce, torn into large pieces
- 2 heads endive, sliced
- 120 ml cherry tomatoes, halved
- 85 g fresh Mozzarella, diced
- Salt and freshly ground black pepper, to taste

Instructions:

1. Slice the pork tenderloin into 1-inch slices. Using a meat pounder, pound the pork slices into thin ½-inch medallions. Generously season the pork with salt and freshly ground black pepper on both sides.
2. Set up a dredging station using three shallow dishes. Put the flour in one dish and the beaten eggs in a second dish. Combine the crushed crackers, paprika, mustard powder, garlic powder, thyme and salt in a third dish.
3. Preheat the air fryer to 204°C.
4. Dredge the pork medallions in flour first and then into the beaten egg. Let the excess egg drip off and coat both sides of the medallions with the cracker crumb mixture. Spray both sides of the coated medallions with vegetable or rapeseed oil.
5. Air fry the medallions in two batches at 204°C for 5 minutes. Once you have air-fried all the medallions, flip them all over and return the first batch of medallions back

into the air fryer on top of the second batch. Air fry at 204°C for an additional 2 minutes.

6. While the medallions are cooking, make the salad and dressing. Whisk the white balsamic vinegar, agave syrup, Dijon mustard, lemon juice, chervil, salt and pepper together in a small bowl. Whisk in the olive oil slowly until combined and thickened.

7. Combine the romaine lettuce, endive, cherry tomatoes, and Mozzarella cheese in a large salad bowl. Drizzle the dressing over the vegetables and toss to combine. Season with salt and freshly ground black pepper.

8. Serve the pork medallions warm on or beside the salad.

Rack of Lamb with Pistachio Crust

Serves 2

Prep time: 10 minutes / Cook time: 19 minutes

Ingredients:

- 120 ml finely chopped pistachios
- 3 tablespoons panko bread crumbs
- 1 teaspoon chopped fresh rosemary
- 2 teaspoons chopped fresh oregano
- Salt and freshly ground black pepper, to taste
- 1 tablespoon olive oil
- 1 rack of lamb, bones trimmed of fat and frenched
- 1 tablespoon Dijon mustard

Instructions:

1. Preheat the air fryer to 192°C.
2. Combine the pistachios, bread crumbs, rosemary, oregano, salt and pepper in a small bowl. (This is a good job for your food processor if you have one.) Drizzle in the olive oil and stir to combine.
3. Season the rack of lamb with salt and pepper on all sides and transfer it to the air fryer basket with the fat side facing up. Air fry the lamb for 12 minutes. Remove the lamb from the air fryer and brush the fat side of the lamb rack with the Dijon mustard. Coat the rack with the pistachio mixture, pressing the bread crumbs onto the lamb with your hands and rolling the bottom of the rack in any of the crumbs that fall off.

4. Return the rack of lamb to the air fryer and air fry for another 3 to 7 minutes or until an instant read thermometer reads 60°C for medium. Add or subtract a couple of minutes for lamb that is more or less well cooked. (Your time will vary depending on how big the rack of lamb is.)

5. Let the lamb rest for at least 5 minutes. Then, slice into chops and serve.

Deconstructed Chicago Dogs

Serves 4

Prep time: 10 minutes / Cook time: 7 minutes

Ingredients:

- 4 hot dogs
- 2 large dill pickles
- 60 ml diced onions
- 1 tomato, cut into ½-inch dice
- 4 pickled or brined jalapeno peppers, diced
- For Garnish (Optional):
- Wholegrain or Dijon mustard
- Celery salt
- Poppy seeds

Instructions:

1. Spray the air fryer basket with avocado oil. Preheat the air fryer to 204°C.
2. Place the hot dogs in the air fryer basket and air fry for 5 to 7 minutes, until hot and slightly crispy.
3. While the hot dogs cook, quarter one of the dill pickles lengthwise, so that you have 4 pickle spears. Finely dice the other pickle.
4. When the hot dogs are done, transfer them to a serving platter and arrange them in a row, alternating with the pickle spears. Top with the

diced pickles, onions, tomato, and jalapeno peppers. Drizzle mustard on top and garnish with celery salt and poppy seeds, if desired.

5. Best served fresh. Store leftover hot dogs in an airtight container in the refrigerator for up to 3 days. Reheat in a preheated 200°C air fryer for 2 minutes, or until warmed through.

Pork and Pinto Bean Gorditas

Prep timePork and Pinto Bean Gorditas

Ingredients:

- 450 g lean pork mince
- 2 tablespoons chili powder
- 2 tablespoons ground cumin
- 1 teaspoon dried oregano
- 2 teaspoons paprika
- 1 teaspoon garlic powder
- 120 ml water
- 1 (425 g) can pinto beans, drained and rinsed
- 120 ml salsa
- Salt and freshly ground black pepper, to taste
- 475 ml grated Cheddar cheese
- 5 (12-inch) flour tortillas
- 4 (8-inch) crispy corn taco shells
- 1 L shredded lettuce
- 1 tomato, diced
- 80 ml sliced black olives
- Sour cream, for serving
- Tomato salsa, for serving
- Cooking spray

Instructions:

1. Preheat the air fryer to 204°C. Spritz the air fryer basket with cooking spray.

2. Put the pork in the air fryer basket and air fry at 204°C for 10 minutes, stirring a few times to gently break up the meat. Combine the chili powder, cumin, oregano, paprika, garlic powder and water in a small bowl. Stir the spice mixture into the browned pork. Stir in the beans and salsa and air fry for an additional minute. Transfer the pork mixture to a bowl. Season with salt and freshly ground black pepper.

3. Sprinkle 120 ml of the grated cheese in the center of the flour tortillas, leaving a 2-inch border around the edge free of cheese and filling. Divide the pork mixture among the four tortillas, placing it on top of the cheese. Put a taco shell on top of the pork and top with shredded lettuce, diced tomatoes, and black olives. Cut the remaining flour tortilla into 4 quarters. These quarters of tortilla will serve as the bottom of the gordita. Put one quarter tortilla on top of each gordita and fold the edges of the bottom flour tortilla up over the sides, enclosing the filling. While holding the seams down, brush the bottom of the gordita with olive oil and place the seam side down on the countertop while you finish the remaining three gorditas.

4. Adjust the temperature to 192°C.

5. Air fry one gordita at a time. Transfer the gordita carefully to the air fryer basket, seam side down. Brush or spray the top tortilla with oil and air fry for 5 minutes. Carefully turn the gordita over and air fry for an additional 4 to 5 minutes until both sides are browned. When finished air frying all four gorditas, layer them back into the air fryer for an additional minute to make sure they are all warm before serving with sour cream and salsa.

Garlic Butter Steak Bites

Serves 3
Prep time: 5 minutes / Cook time: 16 minutes

Ingredients:

- Oil, for spraying
- 450 g boneless steak, cut into 1-inch pieces
- 2 tablespoons olive oil
- 1 teaspoon Worcestershire sauce

- ½ teaspoon granulated garlic
- ½ teaspoon salt
- ¼ teaspoon freshly ground black pepper

Instructions:

1. Preheat the air fryer to 204ºC. Line the air fryer basket with parchment and spray lightly with oil.
2. In a medium bowl, combine the steak, olive oil, Worcestershire sauce, garlic, salt, and black pepper and toss until evenly coated.
3. Place the steak in a single layer in the prepared basket. You may have to work in batches, depending on the size of your air fryer.
4. Cook for 10 to 16 minutes, flipping every 3 to 4 minutes. The total cooking time will depend on the thickness of the meat and your preferred doneness. If you want it well done, it may take up to 5 additional minutes.

Crescent Dogs

Makes 24 crescent dogs

Prep time: 15 minutes / Cook time: 8 minutes

Ingredients:

- Oil, for spraying
- 1 (230 g) can ready-to-bake croissants
- 8 slices Cheddar cheese, cut into thirds
- 24 cocktail sausages or 8 (6-inch) hot dogs, cut into thirds
- 2 tablespoons unsalted butter, melted
- 1 tablespoon sea salt flakes

Instructions:

1. Line the air fryer basket with parchment and spray lightly with oil.
2. Separate the dough into 8 triangles. Cut each triangle into 3 narrow triangles so you have 24 total triangles.
3. Top each triangle with 1 piece of cheese and 1 cocktail sausage.
4. Roll up each piece of dough, starting at the

wide end and rolling toward the point.
5. Place the rolls in the prepared basket in a single layer. You may need to cook in batches, depending on the size of your air fryer.
6. Air fry at 164ºC for 3 to 4 minutes, flip, and cook for another 3 to 4 minutes, or until golden brown.
7. Brush with the melted butter and sprinkle with the sea salt flakes before serving.

Bulgogi Burgers

Serves 4

Prep time: 30 minutes / Cook time: 10 minutes

Ingredients:

- Burgers:
- 450 g 85% lean beef mince
- 60 ml chopped spring onionspring onions
- 2 tablespoons gochujang (Korean red chili paste)
- 1 tablespoon dark soy sauce
- 2 teaspoons minced garlic
- 2 teaspoons minced fresh ginger
- 2 teaspoons sugar
- 1 tablespoon toasted sesame oil
- ½ teaspoon coarse or flaky salt
- Gochujang Mayonnaise:
- 60 ml mayonnaise
- 60 ml chopped spring onionspring onions
- 1 tablespoon gochujang (Korean red chili paste)
- 1 tablespoon toasted sesame oil
- 2 teaspoons sesame seeds
- 4 hamburger buns

Instructions:

1. For the burgers: In a large bowl, mix the ground beef, spring onionspring onions, gochujang, soy sauce, garlic, ginger, sugar, sesame oil, and salt. Marinate at room temperature for 30 minutes, or cover and refrigerate for up to 24 hours.

2. Divide the meat into four portions and form them into round patties. Make a slight depression in the middle of each patty with your thumb to prevent them from puffing up into a dome shape while cooking.

3. Place the patties in a single layer in the air fryer basket. Set the air fryer to 176°C for 10 minutes.

4. Meanwhile, for the gochujang mayonnaise: Stir together the mayonnaise, spring onionspring onions, gochujang, sesame oil, and sesame seeds.

5. At the end of the cooking time, use a meat thermometer to ensure the burgers have reached an internal temperature of 72°C (medium).

6. To serve, place the burgers on the buns and top with the mayonnaise.

Steaks with Walnut-Blue Cheese Butter

Serves 6
Prep time: 30 minutes / Cook time: 10 minutes

Ingredients:

- 120 ml unsalted butter, at room temperature
- 120 ml crumbled blue cheese
- 2 tablespoons finely chopped walnuts
- 1 tablespoon minced fresh rosemary
- 1 teaspoon minced garlic
- ¼ teaspoon cayenne pepper
- Sea salt and freshly ground black pepper, to taste
- 680 g sirloin steaks, at room temperature

Instructions:

1. In a medium bowl, combine the butter, blue cheese, walnuts, rosemary, garlic, and cayenne pepper and salt and black pepper to taste. Use clean hands to ensure that everything is well combined. Place the mixture on a sheet of parchment paper and form it into a log. Wrap it tightly in plastic wrap. Refrigerate for at least 2

hours or freeze for 30 minutes.

2. Season the steaks generously with salt and pepper.

3. Place the air fryer basket or grill pan in the air fryer. Set the air fryer to 204°C and let it preheat for 5 minutes.

4. Place the steaks in the basket in a single layer and air fry for 5 minutes. Flip the steaks, and cook for 5 minutes more, until an instant-read thermometer reads 49°C for medium-rare (or as desired).

5. Transfer the steaks to a plate. Cut the butter into pieces and place the desired amount on top of the steaks. Tent a piece of aluminum foil over the steaks and allow to sit for 10 minutes before serving.

6. Store any remaining butter in a sealed container in the refrigerator for up to 2 weeks.

Spicy Bavette Steak with Zhoug

Serves 4

Prep time: 30 minutes / Cook time: 8 minutes

Ingredients:

- Marinade and Steak:
- 120 ml dark beer or orange juice
- 60 ml fresh lemon juice
- 3 cloves garlic, minced
- 2 tablespoons extra-virgin olive oil
- 2 tablespoons Sriracha
- 2 tablespoons brown sugar
- 2 teaspoons ground cumin
- 2 teaspoons smoked paprika
- 1 tablespoon coarse or flaky salt
- 1 teaspoon black pepper
- 680 g bavette or skirt steak, trimmed and cut into 3 pieces
- Zhoug:
- 235 ml packed fresh coriander leaves
- 2 cloves garlic, peeled
- 2 jalapeño or green chiles, stemmed and

coarsely chopped

- ½ teaspoon ground cumin
- ¼ teaspoon ground coriander
- ¼ teaspoon coarse or flaky salt
- 2 to 4 tablespoons extra-virgin olive oil

Instructions:

1. For the marinade and steak: In a small bowl, whisk together the beer, lemon juice, garlic, olive oil, Sriracha, brown sugar, cumin, paprika, salt, and pepper. Place the steak in a large resealable plastic bag. Pour the marinade over the steak, seal the bag, and massage the steak to coat. Marinate in the refrigerator for 1 hour or up to 24 hours, turning the bag occasionally.

2. Meanwhile, for the zhoug: In a food processor, combine the coriander, garlic, jalapeños, cumin, coriander, and salt. Process until finely chopped. Add 2 tablespoons olive oil and pulse to form a loose paste, adding up to 2 tablespoons more olive oil if needed. Transfer the zhoug to a glass container. Cover and store in the refrigerator until 30 minutes before serving if marinating more than 1 hour.

3. Remove the steak from the marinade and discard the marinade. Place the steak in the air fryer basket and set the air fryer to 204°C for 8 minutes. Use a meat thermometer to ensure the steak has reached an internal temperature of 64°C (for medium).

4. Transfer the steak to a cutting board and let rest for 5 minutes. Slice the steak across the grain and serve with the zhoug.

Steak, Broccoli, and Mushroom Rice Bowls

Serves 4

Prep time: 10 minutes / Cook time: 15 to 18 minutes

Ingredients:

- 2 tablespoons cornflour

- 120 ml low-sodium beef stock
- 1 teaspoon reduced-salt soy sauce
- 340 g rump steak, cut into 1-inch cubes
- 120 ml broccoli florets
- 1 onion, chopped
- 235 ml sliced white or chestnut mushrooms
- 1 tablespoon grated peeled fresh ginger
- Cooked brown rice (optional), for serving

Instructions:

1. In a medium bowl, stir together the cornflour, beef stock, and soy sauce until the cornflour is completely dissolved.

2. Add the beef cubes and toss to coat. Let stand for 5 minutes at room temperature.

3. Insert the crisper plate into the basket and the basket into the unit. Preheat the unit by selecting AIR FRY, setting the temperature to 204°C, and setting the time to 3 minutes. Select START/STOP to begin.

4. Once the unit is preheated, use a slotted spoon to transfer the beef from the stock mixture into a medium metal bowl that fits into the basket. Reserve the stock. Add the broccoli, onion, mushrooms, and ginger to the beef. Place the bowl into the basket.

5. Select AIR FRY, set the temperature to 204°C, and set the time to 18 minutes. Select START/STOP to begin.

6. After about 12 minutes, check the beef and broccoli. If a food thermometer inserted into the beef registers at least 64°C and the vegetables are tender, add the reserved stock and resume cooking for about 3 minutes until the sauce boils. If not, resume cooking for about 3 minutes before adding the reservedstock.

7. When the cooking is complete, serve immediately over hot cooked brown rice, if desired.

Swedish Meatloaf

Serves 8

Prep time: 10 minutes / Cook time: 35 minutes

Ingredients:

- 680 g beef mince (85% lean)
- 110 g pork mince
- 1 large egg (omit for egg-free)
- 120 ml minced onions
- 60 ml tomato sauce
- 2 tablespoons mustard powder
- 2 cloves garlic, minced
- 2 teaspoons fine sea salt
- 1 teaspoon ground black pepper, plus more for garnish

Sauce:

- 120 ml (1 stick) unsalted butter
- 120 ml shredded Swiss or mild Cheddar cheese (about 60 g)
- 60 g cream cheese (60 ml), softened
- 80 ml beef stock
- $\frac{1}{8}$ teaspoon ground nutmeg
- Halved cherry tomatoes, for serving (optional)

Instructions:

1. Preheat the air fryer to 200°C.
2. In a large bowl, combine the beef, pork, egg, onions, tomato sauce, mustard powder, garlic, salt, and pepper. Using your hands, mix until well combined.
3. Place the meatloaf mixture in a loaf pan and place it in the air fryer. Bake for 35 minutes, or until cooked through and the internal temperature reaches 64°C. Check the meatloaf after 25 minutes; if it's getting too brown on the top, cover it loosely with foil to prevent burning.
4. While the meatloaf cooks, make the sauce: Heat the butter in a saucepan over medium-high heat until it sizzles and brown flecks appear, stirring constantly to keep the butter from burning. Turn the heat down to low and whisk in the Swiss cheese, cream cheese, stock, and nutmeg. Simmer for at least 10 minutes. The longer it simmers, the more the flavors open up.
5. When the meatloaf is done, transfer it to a serving tray and pour the sauce over it. Garnish with ground black pepper and serve with cherry tomatoes, if desired. Allow the meatloaf to rest for 10 minutes before slicing so it doesn't crumble apart.
6. Store leftovers in an airtight container in the fridge for 3 days or in the freezer for up to a month. Reheat in a preheated 176°C air fryer for 4 minutes, or until heated through.

Smoky Pork Tenderloin

Serves 6

Prep time: 5 minutes / Cook time: 19 to 22 minutes

Ingredients:

- 680 g pork tenderloin
- 1 tablespoon avocado oil
- 1 teaspoon chili powder
- 1 teaspoon smoked paprika
- 1 teaspoon garlic powder
- 1 teaspoon sea salt
- 1 teaspoon freshly ground black pepper

Instructions:

1. Pierce the tenderloin all over with a fork and rub the oil all over the meat.
2. In a small dish, stir together the chili powder, smoked paprika, garlic powder, salt, and pepper.
3. Rub the spice mixture all over the tenderloin.
4. Set the air fryer to 204°C. Place the pork in the air fryer basket and air fry for 10 minutes. Flip the tenderloin and cook for 9 to 12 minutes more, until an instant-read thermometer reads at least 64°C.
5. Allow the tenderloin to rest for 5 minutes, then slice and serve.

Mongolian-Style Beef

Serves 4

Prep time: 10 minutes / Cook time: 10 minutes

Ingredients:

- Oil, for spraying
- 60 ml cornflour
- 450 g bavette or skirt steak, thinly sliced
- 180 ml packed light brown sugar
- 120 ml soy sauce
- 2 teaspoons toasted sesame oil
- 1 tablespoon minced garlic
- ½ teaspoon ground ginger
- 120 ml water
- Cooked white rice or ramen noodles, for serving

Instructions:

1. Line the air fryer basket with parchment and spray lightly with oil.
2. Place the cornflour in a bowl and dredge the steak until evenly coated. Shake off any excess cornflour.
3. Place the steak in the prepared basket and spray lightly with oil.
4. Roast at 200°C for 5 minutes, flip, and cook for another 5 minutes.
5. In a small saucepan, combine the brown sugar, soy sauce, sesame oil, garlic, ginger, and water and bring to a boil over medium-high heat, stirring frequently. Remove from the heat.
6. Transfer the meat to the sauce and toss until evenly coated. Let sit for about 5 minutes so the steak absorbs the flavors. Serve with white rice or ramen noodles.

Sesame Beef Lettuce Tacos

Serves 4

Prep time: 30 minutes / Cook time: 8 to 10 minutes

Ingredients:

- 60 ml soy sauce or tamari
- 60 ml avocado oil
- 2 tablespoons cooking sherry
- 1 tablespoon granulated sweetener
- 1 tablespoon ground cumin
- 1 teaspoon minced garlic
- Sea salt and freshly ground black pepper, to taste
- 450 g bavette or skirt steak
- 8 butterhead lettuce leaves
- 2 spring onions, sliced
- 1 tablespoon toasted sesame seeds
- Hot sauce, for serving
- Lime wedges, for serving
- Flaky sea salt (optional)

Instructions:

1. In a small bowl, whisk together the soy sauce, avocado oil, cooking sherry, sweetener, cumin, garlic, and salt and pepper to taste.
2. Place the steak in a shallow dish. Pour the marinade over the beef. Cover the dish with plastic wrap and let it marinate in the refrigerator for at least 2 hours or overnight.
3. Remove the flank steak from the dish and discard the marinade.
4. Set the air fryer to 204°C. Place the steak in the air fryer basket and air fry for 4 to 6 minutes. Flip the steak and cook for 4 minutes more, until an instant-read thermometer reads 49°C at the thickest part (or cook it to your desired doneness). Allow the steak to rest for 10 minutes, then slice it thinly against the grain.
5. Stack 2 lettuce leaves on top of each other and add some sliced meat. Top with spring onions and sesame seeds. Drizzle with hot sauce and lime juice, and finish with a little flaky salt (if using). Repeat with the remaining lettuce leaves and fillings.

Chapter 6 Vegetables and Sides

Spiced Honey-Walnut Carrots

Serves 6

Prep time: 5 minutes / Cook time: 12 minutes

Ingredients:

- 450 g baby carrots
- 2 tablespoons olive oil
- 80 g raw honey
- ¼ teaspoon ground cinnamon
- 25 g black walnuts, chopped

Instructions:

1. Preheat the air fryer to 180°C.
2. In a large bowl, toss the baby carrots with olive oil, honey, and cinnamon until well coated.
3. Pour into the air fryer and roast for 6 minutes. Shake the basket, sprinkle the walnuts on top, and roast for 6 minutes more.
4. Remove the carrots from the air fryer and serve.

Easy Rosemary Green Beans

Serves 1

Prep time: 5 minutes / Cook time: 5 minutes

Ingredients:

- 1 tablespoon butter, melted
- 2 tablespoons rosemary
- ½ teaspoon salt
- 3 cloves garlic, minced
- 95 g chopped green beans

Instructions:

1. Preheat the air fryer to 200°C.
2. Combine the melted butter with the rosemary, salt, and minced garlic. Toss in the green beans, coating them well.
3. Air fry for 5 minutes.
4. Serve immediately.

Blistered Shishito Peppers with Lime Juice

Serves 3

Prep time: 5 minutes / Cook time: 9 minutes

Ingredients:

- 230 g shishito peppers, rinsed
- Cooking spray

Sauce:
- 1 tablespoon tamari or shoyu
- 2 teaspoons fresh lime juice
- 2 large garlic cloves, minced

Instructions:

1. Preheat the air fryer to 200°C. Spritz the air fryer basket with cooking spray.
2. Place the shishito peppers in the basket and spritz them with cooking spray. Roast for 3 minutes.
3. Meanwhile, whisk together all the ingredients for the sauce in a large bowl. Set aside.
4. Shake the basket and spritz them with cooking spray again, then roast for an additional 3 minutes.
5. Shake the basket one more time and spray the peppers with cooking spray. Continue roasting for 3 minutes until the peppers are blistered and nicely browned.
6. Remove the peppers from the basket to the bowl of sauce. Toss to coat well and serve immediately.

Citrus Sweet Potatoes and Carrots

Serves 4

Prep time: 5 minutes / Cook time: 20 to 25 minutes

Ingredients:

- 2 large carrots, cut into 1-inch chunks

- 1 medium sweet potato, peeled and cut into 1-inch cubes
- 25 g chopped onion
- 2 garlic cloves, minced
- 2 tablespoons honey
- 1 tablespoon freshly squeezed orange juice
- 2 teaspoons butter, melted

Instructions:

1. Insert the crisper plate into the basket and the basket into the unit. Preheat the unit by selecting AIR ROAST, setting the temperature to 200ºC, and setting the time to 3 minutes. Select START/STOP to begin.
2. In a 6-by-2-inch round pan, toss together the carrots, sweet potato, onion, garlic, honey, orange juice, and melted butter to coat.
3. Once the unit is preheated, place the pan into the basket.
4. Select AIR ROAST, set the temperature to 200ºC, and set the time to 25 minutes. Select START/STOP to begin.
5. After 15 minutes, remove the basket and shake the vegetables. Reinsert the basket to resume cooking. After 5 minutes, if the vegetables are tender and glazed, they are done. If not, resume cooking.
6. When the cooking is complete, serve immediately.

Fig, Chickpea, and Rocket Salad

Serves 4

Prep time: 15 minutes / Cook time: 20 minutes

Ingredients:

- 8 fresh figs, halved
- 250 g cooked chickpeas
- 1 teaspoon crushed roasted cumin seeds
- 4 tablespoons balsamic vinegar
- 2 tablespoons extra-virgin olive oil, plus more for greasing

- Salt and ground black pepper, to taste
- 40 g rocket, washed and dried

Instructions:

1. Preheat the air fryer to 192ºC.
2. Cover the air fryer basket with aluminum foil and grease lightly with oil. Put the figs in the air fryer basket and air fry for 10 minutes.
3. In a bowl, combine the chickpeas and cumin seeds.
4. Remove the air fried figs from the air fryer and replace with the chickpeas. Air fry for 10 minutes. Leave to cool.
5. In the meantime, prepare the dressing. Mix the balsamic vinegar, olive oil, salt and pepper.
6. In a salad bowl, combine the rocket with the cooled figs and chickpeas.
7. Toss with the sauce and serve.

Citrus-Roasted Broccoli Florets

Serves 6

Prep time: 5 minutes / Cook time: 12 minutes

Ingredients:

- 285 g broccoli florets (approximately 1 large head)
- 2 tablespoons olive oil
- ½ teaspoon salt
- 130 ml orange juice
- 1 tablespoon raw honey
- Orange wedges, for serving (optional)

Instructions:

1. Preheat the air fryer to 180ºC.
2. In a large bowl, combine the broccoli, olive oil, salt, orange juice, and honey. Toss the broccoli in the liquid until well coated.
3. Pour the broccoli mixture into the air fryer basket and roast for 6 minutes. Stir and roast for 6 minutes more.
4. Serve alone or with orange wedges for additional citrus flavour, if desired.

Mexican Corn in a Cup

Serves 4

Prep time: 5 minutes / Cook time: 10 minutes

Ingredients:

- 650 g frozen corn kernels (do not thaw)
- Vegetable oil spray
- 2 tablespoons butter
- 60 g sour cream
- 60 g mayonnaise
- 20 g grated Parmesan cheese (or feta, cotija, or queso fresco)
- 2 tablespoons fresh lemon or lime juice
- 1 teaspoon chili powder
- Chopped fresh green onion (optional)
- Chopped fresh coriander (optional)

Instructions:

1. Place the corn in the bottom of the air fryer basket and spray with vegetable oil spray. Set the air fryer to 180°C for 10 minutes.
2. Transfer the corn to a serving bowl. Add the butter and stir until melted. Add the sour cream, mayonnaise, cheese, lemon juice, and chili powder; stir until well combined. Serve immediately with green onion and coriander (if using).

Burger Bun for One

Serves 1

Prep time: 2 minutes / Cook time: 5 minutes

Ingredients:

- 2 tablespoons salted butter, melted
- 25 g blanched finely ground almond flour
- ¼ teaspoon baking powder
- ⅛ teaspoon apple cider vinegar
- 1 large egg, whisked

Instructions:

1. Pour butter into an ungreased ramekin. Add flour, baking powder, and vinegar to ramekin and stir until combined. Add egg and stir until batter is mostly smooth.
2. Place ramekin into air fryer basket. Adjust the temperature to 180°C and bake for 5 minutes. When done, the centre will be firm and the top slightly browned. Let cool, about 5 minutes, then remove from ramekin and slice in half. Serve.

Golden Garlicky Mushrooms

Serves 4

Prep time: 10 minutes / Cook time: 10 minutes

Ingredients:

- 6 small mushrooms
- 1 tablespoon bread crumbs
- 1 tablespoon olive oil
- 30 g onion, peeled and diced
- 1 teaspoon parsley
- 1 teaspoon garlic purée
- Salt and ground black pepper, to taste

Instructions:

1. Preheat the air fryer to 180°C.
2. Combine the bread crumbs, oil, onion, parsley, salt, pepper and garlic in a bowl. Cut out the mushrooms' stalks and stuff each cap with the crumb mixture.
3. Air fry in the air fryer for 10 minutes.
4. Serve hot.

Roasted Grape Tomatoes and Asparagus

Serves 6

Prep time: 5 minutes / Cook time: 12 minutes

Ingredients:

- 400 g grape tomatoes
- 1 bunch asparagus, trimmed

- 2 tablespoons olive oil
- 3 garlic cloves, minced
- ½ teaspoon coarse sea salt

Instructions:

1. Preheat the air fryer to 192ºC.
2. In a large bowl, combine all of the ingredients, tossing until the vegetables are well coated with oil.
3. Pour the vegetable mixture into the air fryer basket and spread into a single layer, then roast for 12 minutes.

Cheesy Loaded Broccoli

Serves 2

Prep time: 10 minutes / Cook time: 10 minutes

Ingredients:

- 215 g fresh broccoli florets
- 1 tablespoon coconut oil
- ¼ teaspoon salt
- 120 g shredded sharp Cheddar cheese
- 60 g sour cream
- 4 slices cooked sugar-free bacon, crumbled
- 1 medium spring onion, trimmed and sliced on the bias

Instructions:

1. Place broccoli into ungreased air fryer basket, drizzle with coconut oil, and sprinkle with salt. Adjust the temperature to 180ºC and roast for 8 minutes. Shake basket three times during cooking to avoid burned spots.
2. Sprinkle broccoli with Cheddar and cook for 2 additional minutes. When done, cheese will be melted and broccoli will be tender.
3. Serve warm in a large serving dish, topped with sour cream, crumbled bacon, and spring onion slices.

Parmesan Herb Focaccia Bread

Serves 6

Prep time: 10 minutes / Cook time: 10 minutes

Ingredients:

- 225 g shredded Mozzarella cheese
- 30 g) full-fat cream cheese
- 95 g blanched finely ground almond flour
- 40 g ground golden flaxseed
- 20 g grated Parmesan cheese
- ½ teaspoon bicarbonate of soda
- 2 large eggs
- ½ teaspoon garlic powder
- ¼ teaspoon dried basil
- ¼ teaspoon dried rosemary
- 2 tablespoons salted butter, melted and divided

Instructions:

1. Place Mozzarella, cream cheese, and almond flour into a large microwave-safe bowl and microwave for 1 minute. Add the flaxseed, Parmesan, and bicarbonate of soda and stir until smooth ball forms. If the mixture cools too much, it will be hard to mix. Return to microwave for 10 to 15 seconds to rewarm if necessary.
2. Stir in eggs. You may need to use your hands to get them fully incorporated. Just keep stirring and they will absorb into the dough.
3. Sprinkle dough with garlic powder, basil, and rosemary and knead into dough. Grease a baking pan with 1 tablespoon melted butter. Press the dough evenly into the pan. Place pan into the air fryer basket.
4. Adjust the temperature to 200ºC and bake for 10 minutes.
5. At 7 minutes, cover with foil if bread begins to get too dark.
6. Remove and let cool at least 30 minutes. Drizzle with remaining butter and serve.

Garlic Cauliflower with Tahini

Serves 4

Prep time: 10 minutes / Cook time: 20 minutes

Ingredients:

Cauliflower:
- 500 g cauliflower florets (about 1 large head)
- 6 garlic cloves, smashed and cut into thirds
- 3 tablespoons vegetable oil
- ½ teaspoon ground cumin
- ½ teaspoon ground coriander
- ½ teaspoon coarse sea salt

Sauce:
- 2 tablespoons tahini (sesame paste)
- 2 tablespoons hot water
- 1 tablespoon fresh lemon juice
- 1 teaspoon minced garlic
- ½ teaspoon coarse sea salt

Instructions:

1. For the cauliflower: In a large bowl, combine the cauliflower florets and garlic. Drizzle with the vegetable oil. Sprinkle with the cumin, coriander, and salt. Toss until well coated.
2. Place the cauliflower in the air fryer basket. Set the air fryer to 200°C for 20 minutes, turning the cauliflower halfway through the cooking time.
3. Meanwhile, for the sauce: In a small bowl, combine the tahini, water, lemon juice, garlic, and salt. (The sauce will appear curdled at first, but keep stirring until you have a thick, creamy, smooth mixture.)
4. Transfer the cauliflower to a large serving bowl. Pour the sauce over and toss gently to coat. Serve immediately.

Lemony Broccoli

Serves 4

Prep time: 10 minutes / Cook time: 9 to 14 minutes per batch

Ingredients:
- 1 large head broccoli, rinsed and patted dry
- 2 teaspoons extra-virgin olive oil
- 1 tablespoon freshly squeezed lemon juice
- Olive oil spray

Instructions:

1. Cut off the broccoli florets and separate them. You can use the stems, too; peel the stems and cut them into 1-inch chunks.
2. Insert the crisper plate into the basket and the basket into the unit. Preheat the unit by selecting AIR ROAST, setting the temperature to 200°C, and setting the time to 3 minutes. Select START/STOP to begin.
3. In a large bowl, toss together the broccoli, olive oil, and lemon juice until coated.
4. Once the unit is preheated, spray the crisper plate with olive oil. Working in batches, place half the broccoli into the basket.
5. Select AIR ROAST, set the temperature to 200°C, and set the time to 14 minutes. Select START/STOP to begin.
6. After 5 minutes, remove the basket and shake the broccoli. Reinsert the basket to resume cooking. Check the broccoli after 5 minutes. If it is crisp-tender and slightly brown around the edges, it is done. If not, resume cooking.
7. When the cooking is complete, transfer the broccoli to a serving bowl. Repeat steps 5 and 6 with the remaining broccoli. Serve immediately.

Lush Vegetable Salad

Serves 4

Prep time: 15 minutes / Cook time: 10 minutes

Ingredients:
- 6 plum tomatoes, halved
- 2 large red onions, sliced
- 4 long red pepper, sliced

- 2 yellow pepper, sliced
- 6 cloves garlic, crushed
- 1 tablespoon extra-virgin olive oil
- 1 teaspoon paprika
- ½ lemon, juiced
- Salt and ground black pepper, to taste
- 1 tablespoon baby capers

Instructions:

1. Preheat the air fryer to 220°C.
2. Put the tomatoes, onions, peppers, and garlic in a large bowl and cover with the extra-virgin olive oil, paprika, and lemon juice. Sprinkle with salt and pepper as desired.
3. Line the inside of the air fryer basket with aluminum foil. Put the vegetables inside and air fry for 10 minutes, ensuring the edges turn brown.
4. Serve in a salad bowl with the baby capers.

Easy Greek Briami (Ratatouille)

Serves 6

Prep time: 15 minutes / Cook time: 40 minutes

Ingredients:

- 2 Maris Piper potatoes, cubed
- 100 g plum tomatoes, cubed
- 1 aubergine, cubed
- 1 courgette, cubed
- 1 red onion, chopped
- 1 red pepper, chopped
- 2 garlic cloves, minced
- 1 teaspoon dried mint
- 1 teaspoon dried parsley
- 1 teaspoon dried oregano
- ½ teaspoon salt
- ½ teaspoon black pepper
- ¼ teaspoon red pepper flakes
- 80 ml olive oil
- 1 (230 g) can tomato paste
- 65 ml vegetable stock
- 65 ml water

Instructions:

1. Preheat the air fryer to 160°C.
2. In a large bowl, combine the potatoes, tomatoes, aubergine, courgette onion, bell pepper, garlic, mint, parsley, oregano, salt, black pepper, and red pepper flakes.
3. In a small bowl, mix together the olive oil, tomato paste, stock, and water.
4. Pour the oil-and-tomato-paste mixture over the vegetables and toss until everything is coated.
5. Pour the coated vegetables into the air fryer basket in an even layer and roast for 20 minutes. After 20 minutes, stir well and spread out again. Roast for an additional 10 minutes, then repeat the process and cook for another 10 minutes.

Cabbage Wedges with Caraway Butter

Serves 6

Prep time: 30 minutes / Cook time: 35 to 40 minutes

Ingredients:

- 1 tablespoon caraway seeds
- 110 g unsalted butter, at room temperature
- ½ teaspoon grated lemon zest
- 1 small head green or red cabbage, cut into 6 wedges
- 1 tablespoon avocado oil
- ½ teaspoon sea salt
- ¼ teaspoon freshly ground black pepper

Instructions:

1. Place the caraway seeds in a small dry skillet over medium-high heat. Toast the seeds for 2 to 3 minutes, then remove them from the heat and let cool. Lightly crush the seeds using a mortar and pestle or with the back of a knife.
2. Place the butter in a small bowl and stir in the crushed caraway seeds and lemon zest.

Form the butter into a log and wrap it in parchment paper or plastic wrap. Refrigerate for at least 1 hour or freeze for 20 minutes.

3. Brush or spray the cabbage wedges with the avocado oil, and sprinkle with the salt and pepper.

4. Set the air fryer to 192ºC. Place the cabbage in a single layer in the air fryer basket and roast for 20 minutes. Flip and cook for 15 to 20 minutes more, until the cabbage is tender and lightly charred. Plate the cabbage and dot with caraway butter. Tent with foil for 5 minutes to melt the butter, and serve.

Garlic Courgette and Red Peppers

Serves 6

Prep time: 5 minutes / Cook time: 15 minutes

Ingredients:

- 2 medium courgette, cubed
- 1 red pepper, diced
- 2 garlic cloves, sliced
- 2 tablespoons olive oil
- ½ teaspoon salt

Instructions:

1. Preheat the air fryer to 193ºC.
2. In a large bowl, mix together the courgette, bell pepper, and garlic with the olive oil and salt.
3. Pour the mixture into the air fryer basket, and roast for 7 minutes. Shake or stir, then roast for 7 to 8 minutes more.

Crispy Lemon Artichoke Hearts

Serves 2

Prep time: 10 minutes / Cook time: 15 minutes

- 1 (425 g) can artichoke hearts in water, drained
- 1 egg
- 1 tablespoon water
- 30 g whole wheat bread crumbs
- ¼ teaspoon salt
- ¼ teaspoon paprika
- ½ lemon

Instructions:

1. Preheat the air fryer to 192ºC.
2. In a medium shallow bowl, beat together the egg and water until frothy.
3. In a separate medium shallow bowl, mix together the bread crumbs, salt, and paprika.
4. Dip each artichoke heart into the egg mixture, then into the bread crumb mixture, coating the outside with the crumbs. Place the artichokes hearts in a single layer of the air fryer basket.
5. Fry the artichoke hearts for 15 minutes.
6. Remove the artichokes from the air fryer, and squeeze fresh lemon juice over the top before serving.

Bacon Potatoes and Green Beans

Serves 4

Prep time: 10 minutes / Cook time: 25 minutes

Ingredients:

- Oil, for spraying
- 900 g medium Maris Piper potatoes, quartered
- 100 g bacon bits
- 280 g fresh green beans
- 1 teaspoon salt
- ½ teaspoon freshly ground black pepper

Instructions:

1. Line the air fryer basket with parchment and spray lightly with oil.

2. Place the potatoes in the prepared basket. Top with the bacon bits and green beans. Sprinkle with the salt and black pepper and spray liberally with oil.
3. Air fry at 180ºC for 25 minutes, stirring after 12 minutes and spraying with oil, until the potatoes are easily pierced with a fork.

Tofu Bites

Serves 4

Prep time: 15 minutes / Cook time: 30 minutes

Ingredients:

- 1 packaged firm tofu, cubed and pressed to remove excess water
- 1 tablespoon soy sauce
- 1 tablespoon ketchup
- 1 tablespoon maple syrup
- ½ teaspoon vinegar
- 1 teaspoon liquid smoke
- 1 teaspoon hot sauce
- 2 tablespoons sesame seeds
- 1 teaspoon garlic powder
- Salt and ground black pepper, to taste
- Cooking spray

Instructions:

1. Preheat the air fryer to 192ºC.
2. Spritz a baking dish with cooking spray.
3. Combine all the ingredients to coat the tofu completely and allow the marinade to absorb for half an hour.
4. Transfer the tofu to the baking dish, then air fry for 15 minutes. Flip the tofu over and air fry for another 15 minutes on the other side.
5. Serve immediately.

Simple Cougette Crisps

Serves 4

Prep time: 5 minutes / Cook time: 14 minutes

Ingredients:

- 2 courgette, sliced into ¼- to ½-inch-thick rounds
- ¼ teaspoon garlic granules
- ⅛ teaspoon sea salt
- Freshly ground black pepper, to taste (optional)
- Cooking spray

Instructions:

1. Preheat the air fryer to 200ºC. Spritz the air fryer basket with cooking spray.
2. Put the courgette rounds in the air fryer basket, spreading them out as much as possible. Top with a sprinkle of garlic granules, sea salt, and black pepper (if desired). Spritz the courgette rounds with cooking spray.
3. Roast for 14 minutes, flipping the courgette rounds halfway through, or until the courgette rounds are crisp-tender.
4. Let them rest for 5 minutes and serve.

Breaded Green Tomatoes

Serves 4

Prep time: 15 minutes / Cook time: 30 minutes

Ingredients:

- 60 g plain flour
- 2 eggs
- 60 g semolina
- 60 g panko bread crumbs
- 1 teaspoon garlic powder
- Salt and freshly ground black pepper, to taste
- 2 green tomatoes, cut into ½-inch-thick rounds
- Cooking oil spray

Instructions:

1. Place the flour in a small bowl.
2. In another small bowl, beat the eggs.
3. In a third small bowl, stir together the semolina, panko, and garlic powder. Season

with salt and pepper.

4. Dip each tomato slice into the flour, the egg, and finally the semolina mixture to coat.

5. Insert the crisper plate into the basket and the basket into the unit. Preheat the unit by selecting AIR FRY, setting the temperature to 200°C, and setting the time to 3 minutes. Select START/STOP to begin.

6. Once the unit is preheated, spray the crisper plate and the basket with cooking oil. Working in batches, place the tomato slices in the air fryer in a single layer. Do not stack them. Spray the tomato slices with the cooking oil.

7. Select AIR FRY, set the temperature to 200°C, and set the time to 10 minutes. Select START/STOP to begin.

8. After 5 minutes, use tongs to flip the tomatoes. Resume cooking for 4 to 5 minutes, or until crisp.

9. When the cooking is complete, transfer the fried green tomatoes to a plate. Repeat steps 6, 7, and 8 for the remaining tomatoes.

Roasted Aubergine

Serves 4

Prep time: 15 minutes / Cook time: 15 minutes

Ingredients:

- 1 large aubergine
- 2 tablespoons olive oil
- ¼ teaspoon salt
- ½ teaspoon garlic powder

Instructions:

1. Remove top and bottom from aubergine.

Slice aubergine into ¼-inch-thick round slices.

2. Brush slices with olive oil. Sprinkle with salt and garlic powder. Place aubergine slices into the air fryer basket.

3. Adjust the temperature to 200°C and set the timer for 15 minutes.

4. Serve immediately.

Rosemary New Potatoes

Serves 4

Prep time: 10 minutes / Cook time: 5 to 6 minutes

Ingredients:

- 3 large red potatoes
- ¼ teaspoon ground rosemary
- ¼ teaspoon ground thyme
- ⅛ teaspoon salt
- ⅛ teaspoon ground black pepper
- 2 teaspoons extra-light olive oil

Instructions:

1. Preheat the air fryer to 170°C. 2. Place potatoes in large bowl and sprinkle with rosemary, thyme, salt, and pepper.

3. Stir with a spoon to distribute seasonings evenly.

4. Add oil to potatoes and stir again to coat well.

5. Air fry at 170°C for 4 minutes. Stir and break apart any that have stuck together.

6. Cook an additional 1 to 2 minutes or until fork-tender.

Chapter 7 Vegetarian Mains

Three-Cheese Courgette Boats

Serves 2

Prep time: 15 minutes / Cook time: 20 minutes

Ingredients:

- 2 medium courgette
- 1 tablespoon avocado oil
- 60 ml low-carb, no-sugar-added pasta sauce
- 60 ml full-fat ricotta cheese
- 60 ml shredded Mozzarella cheese
- ¼ teaspoon dried oregano
- ¼ teaspoon garlic powder
- ½ teaspoon dried parsley
- 2 tablespoons grated vegetarian Parmesan cheese

Instructions:

1. Cut off 1 inch from the top and bottom of each courgette.
2. Slice courgette in half lengthwise and use a spoon to scoop out a bit of the inside, making room for filling.
3. Brush with oil and spoon 2 tablespoons pasta sauce into each shell.
4. In a medium bowl, mix ricotta, Mozzarella, oregano, garlic powder, and parsley. Spoon the mixture into each courgette shell.
5. Place stuffed courgette shells into the air fryer basket.
6. Adjust the temperature to 176°C and air fry for 20 minutes.
7. To remove from the basket, use tongs or a spatula and carefully lift out. Top with Parmesan. Serve immediately.

Mushroom and Pepper Pizza Squares

Serves 10

Prep time: 10 minutes / Cook time: 10 minutes

Ingredients:

- 1 pizza dough, cut into squares
- 235 ml chopped oyster mushrooms
- 1 shallot, chopped
- ¼ red pepper, chopped
- 2 tablespoons parsley
- Salt and ground black pepper, to taste

Instructions:

1. Preheat the air fryer to 204°C.
2. In a bowl, combine the oyster mushrooms, shallot, pepper and parsley.
3. Sprinkle some salt and pepper as desired.
4. Spread this mixture on top of the pizza squares.
5. Bake in the air fryer for 10 minutes.
6. Serve warm.

Stuffed Portobellos

Serves 4

Prep time: 10 minutes / Cook time: 8 minutes

Ingredients:

- 85 g soft white cheese
- ½ medium courgette, trimmed and chopped
- 60 ml seeded and chopped red pepper
- 350 ml chopped fresh spinach leaves
- 4 large portobello mushrooms, stems removed
- 2 tablespoons coconut oil, melted
- ½ teaspoon salt

Instructions:

1. In a medium bowl, mix soft white cheese, courgette, pepper, and spinach.
2. Drizzle mushrooms with coconut oil and sprinkle with salt.
3. Scoop ¼ courgette mixture into each mushroom.
4. Place mushrooms into ungreased air fryer basket.
5. Adjust the temperature to 204°C and air fry for 8 minutes.
6. Portobellos will be tender, and tops will be browned when done.
7. Serve warm.

Broccoli Crust Pizza

Serves 4

Prep time: 15 minutes / Cook time: 12 minutes

Ingredients:

- 700 ml riced broccoli, steamed and drained well
- 1 large egg
- 120 ml grated vegetarian Parmesan cheese
- 3 tablespoons low-carb Alfredo sauce
- 120 ml shredded Mozzarella cheese

Instructions:

1. In a large bowl, mix broccoli, egg, and Parmesan.
2. Cut a piece of parchment to fit your air fryer basket.
3. Press out the pizza mixture to fit on the parchment, working in two batches if necessary.
4. Place into the air fryer basket. Adjust the temperature to 188°C and air fry for 5 minutes.
5. The crust should be firm enough to flip. If not, add 2 additional minutes.
6. Flip crust. Top with Alfredo sauce and Mozzarella. Return to the air fryer basket and cook an additional 7 minutes or until cheese is golden and bubbling.
7. Serve warm.

Tangy Asparagus and Broccoli

Serves 4

Prep time: 25 minutes / Cook time: 22 minutes

Ingredients:

- 230 g asparagus, cut into 1½-inch pieces
- 230 g broccoli, cut into 1½-inch pieces
- 2 tablespoons olive oil
- Salt and white pepper, to taste
- 120 ml vegetable broth
- 2 tablespoons apple cider vinegar

Instructions:

1. Place the vegetables in a single layer in the lightly greased air fryer basket.
2. Drizzle the olive oil over the vegetables. Sprinkle with salt and white pepper.
3. Cook at 192°C for 15 minutes, shaking the basket halfway through the cooking time.
4. Add 120 ml of vegetable broth to a saucepan; bring to a rapid boil and add the vinegar.
5. Cook for 5 to 7 minutes or until the sauce has reduced by half.

6. Spoon the sauce over the warm vegetables and serve immediately.

Roasted Veggie Bowl

Serves 2

Prep time: 10 minutes / Cook time: 15 minutes

Ingredients:

- 235 ml broccoli florets
- 235 ml quartered Brussels sprouts
- 120 ml cauliflower florets
- ¼ medium white onion, peeled and sliced ¼ inch thick
- ½ medium green pepper, seeded and sliced ¼ inch thick
- 1 tablespoon coconut oil
- 2 teaspoons chilli powder
- ½ teaspoon garlic powder
- ½ teaspoon cumin

Instructions:

1. Toss all ingredients together in a large bowl until vegetables are fully coated with oil and seasoning.
2. Pour vegetables into the air fryer basket.
3. Adjust the temperature to 182°C and roast for 15 minutes.
4. Shake two or three times during cooking.
5. Serve warm.

Broccoli with Garlic Sauce

Serves 4

Prep time: 19 minutes / Cook time: 15 minutes

Ingredients:

- 2 tablespoons olive oil
- Rock salt and freshly ground black pepper, to taste
- 450 g broccoli florets
- Dipping Sauce:

- 2 teaspoons dried rosemary, crushed
- 3 garlic cloves, minced
- ⅓ teaspoon dried marjoram, crushed
- 60 ml sour cream
- 80 ml mayonnaise

Instructions:

1. Lightly grease your broccoli with a thin layer of olive oil.
2. Season with salt and ground black pepper.
3. Arrange the seasoned broccoli in the air fryer basket.
4. Bake at 202°C for 15 minutes, shaking once or twice.
5. In the meantime, prepare the dipping sauce by mixing all the sauce ingredients.
6. Serve warm broccoli with the dipping sauce and enjoy!

Pesto Vegetable Skewers

Makes 8 skewers

Prep time: 30 minutes / Cook time: 8 minutes

Ingredients:

- 1 medium courgette, trimmed and cut into ½-inch slices
- ½ medium brown onion, peeled and cut into 1-inch squares
- 1 medium red pepper, seeded and cut into 1-inch squares
- 16 whole cremini or chestnut mushrooms
- 80 ml basil pesto
- ½ teaspoon salt
- ¼ teaspoon ground black pepper

Instructions:

1. Divide courgette slices, onion, and pepper into eight even portions.
2. Place on 6-inch skewers for a total of eight kebabs.
3. Add 2 mushrooms to each skewer and brush

kebabs generously with pesto.

4. Sprinkle each kebab with salt and black pepper on all sides, then place into ungreased air fryer basket.

5. Adjust the temperature to 192ºC and air fry for 8 minutes, turning kebabs halfway through cooking.

6. Vegetables will be browned at the edges and tender-crisp when done.

7. Serve warm.

Fried Root Vegetable Medley with Thyme

Serves 4

Prep time: 10 minutes / Cook time: 22 minutes

Ingredients:

- 2 carrots, sliced
- 2 potatoes, cut into chunks
- 1 swede, cut into chunks
- 1 turnip, cut into chunks
- 1 beetroot, cut into chunks
- 8 shallots, halved
- 2 tablespoons olive oil
- Salt and black pepper, to taste
- 2 tablespoons tomato pesto
- 2 tablespoons water
- 2 tablespoons chopped fresh thyme

Instructions:

1. Preheat the air fryer to 204ºC.

2. Toss the carrots, potatoes, swede, turnip, beetroot, shallots, olive oil, salt, and pepper in a large mixing bowl until the root vegetables are evenly coated.

3. Place the root vegetables in the air fryer basket and air fry for 12 minutes.

4. Shake the basket and air fry for another 10 minutes until they are cooked to your preferred doneness.

5. Meanwhile, in a small bowl, whisk together the tomato pesto and water until smooth.

6. When ready, remove the root vegetables from the basket to a platter.

7. Drizzle with the tomato pesto mixture and sprinkle with the thyme. Serve immediately.

Spinach-Artichoke Stuffed Mushrooms

Serves 4

Prep time: 10 minutes / Cook time: 10 to 14 minutes

Ingredients:

- 2 tablespoons olive oil
- 4 large portobello mushrooms, stems removed and gills scraped out
- ½ teaspoon salt
- ¼ teaspoon freshly ground pepper
- 110 g goat cheese, crumbled
- 120 ml chopped marinated artichoke hearts
- 235 ml frozen spinach, thawed and squeezed dry
- 120 ml grated Parmesan cheese
- 2 tablespoons chopped fresh parsley

Instructions:

1. Preheat the air fryer to 204ºC.

2. Rub the olive oil over the portobello mushrooms until thoroughly coated.

3. Sprinkle both sides with the salt and black pepper.

4. Place top-side down on a clean work surface.

5. In a small bowl, combine the goat cheese, artichoke hearts, and spinach.

6. Mash with the back of a fork until thoroughly combined.

7. Divide the cheese mixture among the mushrooms and sprinkle with the Parmesan cheese.

8. Air fry for 10 to 14 minutes until the mushrooms are tender and the cheese has begun to brown.

9. Top with the fresh parsley just before serving.

Chapter 8 Snacks and Appetizers

Poutine with Waffle Fries

Serves 4

Prep time: 10 minutes / Cook time: 15 to 17 minutes

Ingredients:
- 475 ml frozen waffle cut fries
- 2 teaspoons olive oil
- 1 red pepper, chopped
- 2 spring onions, sliced
- 240 ml shredded Swiss cheese
- 120 ml bottled chicken gravy

Instructions:
1. Preheat the air fryer to 192ºC.
2. Toss the waffle fries with the olive oil and place in the air fryer basket. Air fry for 10 to 12 minutes, or until the fries are crisp and light golden brown, shaking the basket halfway through the cooking time.
3. Transfer the fries to a baking pan and top with the pepper, spring onions, and cheese. Air fry for 3 minutes, or until the vegetables are crisp and tender.
4. Remove the pan from the air fryer and drizzle the gravy over the fries. Air fry for 2 minutes, or until the gravy is hot.
5. Serve immediately.

Courgette Feta Roulades

Serves 6

Prep time: 10 minutes / Cook time: 10 minutes

Ingredients:
- 120 ml feta
- 1 garlic clove, minced
- 2 tablespoons fresh basil, minced
- 1 tablespoon capers, minced
- ⅛ teaspoon salt
- ⅛ teaspoon red pepper flakes
- 1 tablespoon lemon juice
- 2 medium courgette
- 12 toothpicks

Instructions:
1. Preheat the air fryer to 182ºC. (If using a grill attachment, make sure it is inside the air fryer during preheating.)
2. In a small bowl, combine the feta, garlic, basil, capers, salt, red pepper flakes, and lemon juice.
3. Slice the courgette into ⅛-inch strips lengthwise. (Each courgette should yield around 6 strips.)
4. Spread 1 tablespoon of the cheese filling onto each slice of courgette, then roll it up and secure it with a toothpick through the middle.
5. Place the courgette roulades into the air fryer basket in a single layer, making sure that they don't touch each other.
6. Bake or grill in the air fryer for 10 minutes.
7. Remove the courgette roulades from the air fryer and gently remove the toothpicks before serving.

Lebanese Muhammara

Serves 6

Prep time: 15 minutes / Cook time: 15 minutes

Ingredients:
- 2 large red peppers
- 60 ml plus 2 tablespoons extra-virgin olive oil
- 240 ml walnut halves
- 1 tablespoon agave nectar or honey

- 1 teaspoon fresh lemon juice
- 1 teaspoon ground cumin
- 1 teaspoon rock salt
- 1 teaspoon red pepper flakes
- Raw vegetables (such as cucumber, carrots, courgette slices, or cauliflower) or toasted pitta chips, for serving

Instructions:

1. Drizzle the peppers with 2 tablespoons of the olive oil and place in the air fryer basket. Set the air fryer to 204°C for 10 minutes.
2. Add the walnuts to the basket, arranging them around the peppers. Set the air fryer to 204°C for 5 minutes.
3. Remove the peppers, seal in a resealable plastic bag, and let rest for 5 to 10 minutes. Transfer the walnuts to a plate and set aside to cool.
4. Place the softened peppers, walnuts, agave, lemon juice, cumin, salt, and ½ teaspoon of the pepper flakes in a food processor and purée until smooth.
5. Transfer the dip to a serving bowl and make an indentation in the middle. Pour the remaining 60 ml olive oil into the indentation. Garnish the dip with the remaining ½ teaspoon pepper flakes.
6. Serve with vegetables or toasted pitta chips.

Bacon-Wrapped Shrimp and Jalapeño

Serves 8

Prep time: 20 minutes / Cook time: 26 minutes

Ingredients:

- 24 large shrimp, peeled and deveined, about 340 g
- 5 tablespoons barbecue sauce, divided
- 12 strips bacon, cut in half
- 24 small pickled jalapeño slices

Instructions:

1. Toss together the shrimp and 3 tablespoons of the barbecue sauce. Let stand for 15 minutes. Soak 24 wooden toothpicks in water for 10 minutes. Wrap 1 piece bacon around the shrimp and jalapeño slice, then secure with a toothpick.
2. Preheat the air fryer to 176°C.
3. Working in batches, place half of the shrimp in the air fryer basket, spacing them ½ inch apart. Air fry for 10 minutes. Turn shrimp over with tongs and air fry for 3 minutes more, or until bacon is golden brown and shrimp are cooked through.
4. Brush with the remaining barbecue sauce and serve.

Stuffed Fried Mushrooms

Serves 10

Prep time: 20 minutes / Cook time: 10 to 11 minutes

Ingredients:

- 120 ml panko breadcrumbs
- ½ teaspoon freshly ground black pepper
- ½ teaspoon onion powder
- ½ teaspoon cayenne pepper
- 1 (227 g) package soft white cheese, at room temperature
- 20 cremini or button mushrooms, stemmed
- 1 to 2 tablespoons oil

Instructions:

1. In a medium bowl, whisk the breadcrumbs, black pepper, onion powder, and cayenne until blended.
2. Add the soft white cheese and mix until well blended. Fill each mushroom top with 1 teaspoon of the soft white cheese mixture
3. Preheat the air fryer to 182°C. Line the air fryer basket with a piece of parchment paper.
4. Place the mushrooms on the parchment and

spritz with oil.

5. Cook for 5 minutes. Shake the basket and cook for 5 to 6 minutes more until the filling is firm and the mushrooms are soft.

Bacon-Wrapped Pickle Spears

Serves 4

Prep time: 10 minutes / Cook time: 8 minutes

Ingredients:

- 8 to 12 slices bacon
- 60 ml soft white cheese
- 60 ml shredded Mozzarella cheese
- 8 dill pickle spears
- 120 ml ranch dressing

Instructions:

1. Lay the bacon slices on a flat surface. In a medium bowl, combine the soft white cheese and Mozzarella. Stir until well blended. Spread the cheese mixture over the bacon slices.

2. Place a pickle spear on a bacon slice and roll the bacon around the pickle in a spiral, ensuring the pickle is fully covered. (You may need to use more than one slice of bacon per pickle to fully cover the spear.) Tuck in the ends to ensure the bacon stays put. Repeat to wrap all the pickles.

3. Place the wrapped pickles in the air fryer basket in a single layer. Set the air fryer to 204ºC for 8 minutes, or until the bacon is cooked through and crisp on the edges.

4. Serve the pickle spears with ranch dressing on the side.

Shishito Peppers with Herb Dressing

Serves 2 to 4

Prep time: 10 minutes / Cook time: 6 minutes

Ingredients:

- 170 g shishito or Padron peppers
- 1 tablespoon vegetable oil
- Rock salt and freshly ground black pepper, to taste
- 120 ml mayonnaise
- 2 tablespoons finely chopped fresh basil leaves
- 2 tablespoons finely chopped fresh flat-leaf parsley
- 1 tablespoon finely chopped fresh tarragon
- 1 tablespoon finely chopped fresh chives
- Finely grated zest of ½ lemon
- 1 tablespoon fresh lemon juice
- Flaky sea salt, for serving

Instructions:

1. Preheat the air fryer to 204ºC.

2. In a bowl, toss together the shishitos and oil to evenly coat and season with rock salt and black pepper. Transfer to the air fryer and air fry for 6 minutes, shaking the basket halfway through, or until the shishitos are blistered and lightly charred.

3. Meanwhile, in a small bowl, whisk together the mayonnaise, basil, parsley, tarragon, chives, lemon zest, and lemon juice.

4. Pile the peppers on a plate, sprinkle with flaky sea salt, and serve hot with the dressing.

Classic Spring Rolls

Makes 16 spring rolls

Prep time: 10 minutes / Cook time: 9 minutes

Ingredients:

- 4 teaspoons toasted sesame oil
- 6 medium garlic cloves, minced or pressed
- 1 tablespoon grated peeled fresh ginger
- 475 ml thinly sliced shiitake mushrooms
- 1 L chopped green cabbage

- 240 ml grated carrot
- ½ teaspoon sea salt
- 16 rice paper wrappers
- Cooking oil spray (sunflower, safflower, or refined coconut)
- Gluten-free sweet and sour sauce or Thai sweet chilli sauce, for serving (optional)

Instructions:

1. Place a wok or sauté pan over medium heat until hot.
2. Add the sesame oil, garlic, ginger, mushrooms, cabbage, carrot, and salt. Cook for 3 to 4 minutes, stirring often, until the cabbage is lightly wilted. Remove the pan from the heat.
3. Gently run a rice paper under water. Lay it on a flat non-absorbent surface. Place about 60 ml of the cabbage filling in the middle. Once the wrapper is soft enough to roll, fold the bottom up over the filling, fold in the sides, and roll the wrapper all the way up. (Basically, make a tiny burrito.)
4. Repeat step 3 to make the remaining spring rolls until you have the number of spring rolls you want to cook right now (and the amount that will fit in the air fryer basket in a single layer without them touching each other). Refrigerate any leftover filling in an airtight container for about 1 week.
5. Insert the crisper plate into the basket and the basket into the unit. Preheat the unit by selecting AIR FRY, setting the temperature to 200°C, and setting the time to 3 minutes. Select START/STOP to begin.
6. Once the unit is preheated, spray the crisper plate and the basket with cooking oil. Place the spring rolls into the basket, leaving a little room between them so they don't stick to each other. Spray the top of each spring roll with cooking oil.
7. Select AIR FRY, set the temperature to 200°C, and set the time to 9 minutes. Select START/STOP to begin.
8. When the cooking is complete, the egg rolls should be crisp-ish and lightly browned. Serve immediately, plain or with a sauce of choice.

Mushroom Tarts

Makes 15 tarts

Prep time: 15 minutes / Cook time: 38 minutes

Ingredients:

- 2 tablespoons extra-virgin olive oil, divided
- 1 small white onion, sliced
- 227 g shiitake mushrooms, sliced
- ¼ teaspoon sea salt
- ¼ teaspoon freshly ground black pepper
- 60 ml dry white wine
- 1 sheet frozen puff pastry, thawed
- 240 ml shredded Gruyère cheese
- Cooking oil spray
- 1 tablespoon thinly sliced fresh chives

Instructions:

1. Insert the crisper plate into the basket and the basket into the unit. Preheat the unit by selecting BAKE, setting the temperature to 148°C, and setting the time to 3 minutes. Select START/STOP to begin.
2. In a heatproof bowl that fits into the basket, stir together 1 tablespoon of olive oil, the onion, and the mushrooms.
3. Once the unit is preheated, place the bowl into the basket.
4. Select BAKE, set the temperature to 148°C, and set the time to 7 minutes. Select START/STOP to begin.
5. After about 2½ minutes, stir the vegetables. Resume cooking. After another 2½ minutes, the vegetables should be browned and tender. Season with the salt and pepper and

add the wine. Resume cooking until the liquid evaporates, about 2 minutes.

6. When the cooking is complete, place the bowl on a heatproof surface.

7. Increase the air fryer temperature to 200ºC and set the time to 3 minutes. Select START/ STOP to begin.

8. Unfold the puff pastry and cut it into 15 (3-by-3-inch) squares. Using a fork, pierce the dough and brush both sides with the remaining 1 tablespoon of olive oil.

9. Evenly distribute half the cheese among the puff pastry squares, leaving a ½-inch border around the edges. Divide the mushroom-onion mixture among the pastry squares and top with the remaining cheese.

10. Once the unit is preheated, spray the crisper plate with cooking oil. Working in batches, place 5 tarts into the basket; do not stack or overlap.

11. Select BAKE, set the temperature to 200ºC, and set the time to 8 minutes. Select START/ STOP to begin.

12. After 6 minutes, check the tarts; if not yet golden brown, resume cooking for about 2 minutes more.

13. When the cooking is complete, remove the tarts and transfer to a wire rack to cool. Repeat steps 10, 11, and 12 with the remaining tarts.

14. Serve garnished with the chives.

Lemony Endive in Curried Yoghurt

Serves 6

Prep time: 5 minutes / Cook time: 10 minutes

Ingredients:

- 6 heads endive
- 120 ml plain and fat-free yoghurt
- 3 tablespoons lemon juice
- 1 teaspoon garlic powder
- ½ teaspoon curry powder
- Salt and ground black pepper, to taste

Instructions:

1. Wash the endives and slice them in half lengthwise.

2. In a bowl, mix together the yoghurt, lemon juice, garlic powder, curry powder, salt and pepper.

3. Brush the endive halves with the marinade, coating them completely. Allow to sit for at least 30 minutes or up to 24 hours.

4. Preheat the air fryer to 160ºC.

5. Put the endives in the air fryer basket and air fry for 10 minutes.

6. Serve hot.

Greek Potato Skins with Olives and Feta

Serves 4

Prep time: 5 minutes / Cook time: 45 minutes

Ingredients:

- 2 russet or Maris Piper potatoes
- 3 tablespoons olive oil, divided, plus more for drizzling (optional)
- 1 teaspoon rock salt, divided
- ¼ teaspoon black pepper
- 2 tablespoons fresh coriander, chopped, plus more for serving
- 60 ml Kalamata olives, diced
- 60 ml crumbled feta
- Chopped fresh parsley, for garnish (optional)

Instructions:

1. Preheat the air fryer to 192ºC.

2. Using a fork, poke 2 to 3 holes in the potatoes, then coat each with about ½ tablespoon olive oil and ½ teaspoon salt.

3. Place the potatoes into the air fryer basket and bake for 30 minutes.

4. Remove the potatoes from the air fryer, and slice in half. Using a spoon, scoop out the flesh of the potatoes, leaving a ½-inch layer of potato inside the skins, and set the skins aside.

5. In a medium bowl, combine the scooped potato middles with the remaining 2 tablespoons of olive oil, ½ teaspoon of salt, black pepper, and coriander. Mix until well combined.

6. Divide the potato filling into the now-empty potato skins, spreading it evenly over them. Top each potato with a tablespoon each of the olives and feta.

7. Place the loaded potato skins back into the air fryer and bake for 15 minutes.

8. Serve with additional chopped coriander or parsley and a drizzle of olive oil, if desired.

Garlicky and Cheesy French Fries

Serves 4

Prep time: 5 minutes / Cook time: 20 to 25 minutes

Ingredients:

- 3 medium russet or Maris Piper potatoes, rinsed, dried, and cut into thin wedges or classic fry shapes
- 2 tablespoons extra-virgin olive oil
- 1 tablespoon granulated garlic
- 80 ml grated Parmesan cheese
- ½ teaspoon salt
- ¼ teaspoon freshly ground black pepper
- Cooking oil spray
- 2 tablespoons finely chopped fresh parsley (optional)

Instructions:

1. In a large bowl combine the potato wedges or fries and the olive oil. Toss to coat.

2. Sprinkle the potatoes with the granulated

garlic, Parmesan cheese, salt, and pepper, and toss again.

3. Insert the crisper plate into the basket and the basket into the unit. Preheat the unit by selecting AIR FRY, setting the temperature to 204°C, and setting the time to 3 minutes. Select START/STOP to begin.

4. Once the unit is preheated, spray the crisper plate with cooking oil. Place the potatoes into the basket.

5. Select AIR FRY, set the temperature to 204°C, and set the time to 20 to 25 minutes. Select START/STOP to begin.

6. After about 10 minutes, remove the basket and shake it so the fries at the bottom come up to the top. Reinsert the basket to resume cooking.

7. When the cooking is complete, top the fries with the parsley (if using) and serve hot.

Sea Salt Potato Crisps

Serves 4

Prep time: 30 minutes / Cook time: 27 minutes

Ingredients:

- Oil, for spraying
- 4 medium yellow potatoes such as Maris Pipers
- 1 tablespoon oil
- ⅛ to ¼ teaspoon fine sea salt

Instructions:

1. Line the air fryer basket with parchment and spray lightly with oil.

2. Using a mandoline or a very sharp knife, cut the potatoes into very thin slices.

3. Place the slices in a bowl of cold water and let soak for about 20 minutes.

4. Drain the potatoes, transfer them to a plate lined with paper towels, and pat dry.

5. Drizzle the oil over the potatoes, sprinkle with the salt, and toss to combine. Transfer

to the prepared basket.

6. Air fry at 92°C for 20 minutes. Toss the crisps, increase the heat to 204°C, and cook for another 5 to 7 minutes, until crispy.

Shrimp Toasts with Sesame Seeds

Serves 4 to 6

Prep time: 15 minutes / Cook time: 6 to 8 minutes

Ingredients:

- 230 g raw shrimp, peeled and deveined
- 1 egg, beaten
- 2 spring onions, chopped, plus more for garnish
- 2 tablespoons chopped fresh coriander
- 2 teaspoons grated fresh ginger
- 1 to 2 teaspoons sriracha sauce
- 1 teaspoon soy sauce
- ½ teaspoon toasted sesame oil
- 6 slices thinly sliced white sandwich bread
- 120 ml sesame seeds
- Cooking spray
- Thai chilli sauce, for serving

Instructions:

1. Preheat the air fryer to 204°C. Spritz the air fryer basket with cooking spray.
2. In a food processor, add the shrimp, egg, spring onions, coriander, ginger, sriracha sauce, soy sauce and sesame oil, and pulse until chopped finely. You'll need to stop the food processor occasionally to scrape down the sides. Transfer the shrimp mixture to a bowl.
3. On a clean work surface, cut the crusts off the sandwich bread. Using a brush, generously brush one side of each slice of bread with shrimp mixture.
4. Place the sesame seeds on a plate. Press bread slices, shrimp-side down, into sesame seeds to coat evenly. Cut each slice

diagonally into quarters.

5. Spread the coated slices in a single layer in the air fryer basket.
6. Air fry in batches for 6 to 8 minutes, or until golden and crispy. Flip the bread slices halfway through. Repeat with the remaining bread slices.
7. Transfer to a plate and let cool for 5 minutes. Top with the chopped spring onions and serve warm with Thai chilli sauce.

Crispy Mozzarella Sticks

Serves 4

Prep time: 8 minutes / Cook time: 5 minutes

Ingredients:

- 120 ml plain flour
- 1 egg, beaten
- 120 ml panko breadcrumbs
- 120 ml grated Parmesan cheese
- 1 teaspoon Italian seasoning
- ½ teaspoon garlic salt
- 6 Mozzarella sticks, halved crosswise
- Olive oil spray

Instructions:

1. Put the flour in a small bowl.
2. Put the beaten egg in another small bowl.
3. In a medium bowl, stir together the panko, Parmesan cheese, Italian seasoning, and garlic salt.
4. Roll a Mozzarella-stick half in the flour, dip it into the egg, and then roll it in the panko mixture to coat. Press the coating lightly to make sure the breadcrumbs stick to the cheese. Repeat with the remaining 11 Mozzarella sticks.
5. Insert the crisper plate into the basket and the basket into the unit. Preheat the unit by selecting AIR FRY, setting the temperature to 204°C, and setting the time to 3 minutes.

Select START/STOP to begin.

6. Once the unit is preheated, spray the crisper plate with olive oil and place a parchment paper liner in the basket. Place the Mozzarella sticks into the basket and lightly spray them with olive oil.

7. Select AIR FRY, set the temperature to 204°C, and set the time to 5 minutes. Select START/STOP to begin.

8. When the cooking is complete, the Mozzarella sticks should be golden and crispy. Let the sticks stand for 1 minute before transferring them to a serving plate. Serve warm.

Kale Chips with Tex-Mex Dip

Serves 8

Prep time: 10 minutes / Cook time: 5 to 6 minutes

Ingredients:

- 240 ml Greek yoghurt
- 1 tablespoon chilli powder
- 80 ml low-salt salsa, well drained
- 1 bunch curly kale
- 1 teaspoon olive oil
- ¼ teaspoon coarse sea salt

Instructions:

1. In a small bowl, combine the yoghurt, chilli powder, and drained salsa; refrigerate.

2. Rinse the kale thoroughly, and pat dry. Remove the stems and ribs from the kale, using a sharp knife. Cut or tear the leaves into 3-inch pieces.

3. Toss the kale with the olive oil in a large bowl.

4. Air fry the kale in small batches at 200°C until the leaves are crisp. This should take 5 to 6 minutes. Shake the basket once during cooking time.

5. As you remove the kale chips, sprinkle them

with a bit of the sea salt.

6. When all of the kale chips are done, serve with the dip.

String Bean Fries

Serves 4

Prep time: 15 minutes / Cook time: 5 to 6 minutes

Ingredients:

Ingredients:

- 227 g fresh green beans
- 2 eggs
- 4 teaspoons water
- 120 ml white flour
- 120 ml breadcrumbs
- ¼ teaspoon salt
- ¼ teaspoon ground black pepper
- ¼ teaspoon mustard powder (optional)
- Oil for misting or cooking spray

Instructions:

1. Preheat the air fryer to 182°C.

2. Trim stem ends from green beans, wash, and pat dry.

3. In a shallow dish, beat eggs and water together until well blended.

4. Place flour in a second shallow dish.

5. In a third shallow dish, stir together the breadcrumbs, salt, pepper, and dry mustard if using.

6. Dip each bean in egg mixture, flour, egg mixture again, then breadcrumbs.

7. When you finish coating all the green beans, open air fryer and place them in basket.

8. Cook for 3 minutes.

9. Stop and mist green beans with oil or cooking spray.

10. Cook for 2 to 3 more minutes or until green beans are crispy and nicely browned.

Ranch Oyster Snack Crackers

Serves 6

Prep time: 3 minutes / Cook time: 12 minutes

Ingredients:

- Oil, for spraying
- 60 ml olive oil
- 2 teaspoons dry ranch seasoning
- 1 teaspoon chilli powder
- ½ teaspoon dried dill
- ½ teaspoon granulated garlic
- ½ teaspoon salt
- 1 (255 g) bag oyster crackers or low-salt crackers

Instructions:

1. Preheat the air fryer to 164°C. Line the air fryer basket with parchment and spray lightly with oil.
2. In a large bowl, mix together the olive oil, ranch seasoning, chilli powder, dill, garlic, and salt. Add the crackers and toss until evenly coated.
3. Place the mixture in the prepared basket.
4. Cook for 10 to 12 minutes, shaking or stirring every 3 to 4 minutes, or until crisp and golden brown.

Carrot Chips

Serves 4

Prep time: 15 minutes / Cook time: 8 to 10 minutes

Ingredients:

- 1 tablespoon olive oil, plus more for greasing the basket
- 4 to 5 medium carrots, trimmed and thinly sliced
- 1 teaspoon seasoned salt

Instructions:

1. Preheat the air fryer to 200°C. Grease the air fryer basket with the olive oil.
2. Toss the carrot slices with 1 tablespoon of olive oil and salt in a medium bowl until thoroughly coated.
3. Arrange the carrot slices in the greased basket. You may need to work in batches to avoid overcrowding.
4. Air fry for 8 to 10 minutes until the carrot slices are crisp-tender. Shake the basket once during cooking.
5. Transfer the carrot slices to a bowl and repeat with the remaining carrots.
6. Allow to cool for 5 minutes and serve.

Spiced Roasted Cashews

Serves 4

Prep time: 5 minutes / Cook time: 10 minutes

Ingredients:

- 475 ml raw cashews
- 2 tablespoons olive oil
- ¼ teaspoon salt
- ¼ teaspoon chilli powder
- ⅛ teaspoon garlic powder
- ⅛ teaspoon smoked paprika

Instructions:

1. Preheat the air fryer to 182°C.
2. In a large bowl, toss all of the ingredients together.
3. Pour the cashews into the air fryer basket and roast them for 5 minutes. Shake the basket, then cook for 5 minutes more.
4. Serve immediately.

Chapter 9 Desserts

Almond-Roasted Pears

Serves 4

Prep time: 10 minutes / Cook time: 15 to 20 minutes

Ingredients:

- Yogurt Topping:
- 140-170 g pot vanilla Greek yogurt
- ¼ teaspoon almond flavoring
- 2 whole pears
- 4 crushed Biscoff biscuits
- 1 tablespoon flaked almonds
- 1 tablespoon unsalted butter

Instructions:

1. Stir the almond flavoring into yogurt and set aside while preparing pears.
2. Halve each pear and spoon out the core.
3. Place pear halves in air fryer basket, skin side down.
4. Stir together the crushed biscuits and almonds. Place a quarter of this mixture into the hollow of each pear half.
5. Cut butter into 4 pieces and place one piece on top of biscuit mixture in each pear.
6. Roast at 184°C for 15 to 20 minutes, or until pears have cooked through but are still slightly firm.
7. Serve pears warm with a dollop of yogurt topping.

Vanilla and Cardamon Walnuts Tart

Serves 6

Prep time: 5 minutes / Cook time: 13 minutes

Ingredients:

- 240 ml coconut milk
- 60 g walnuts, ground
- 60 g powdered sweetener
- 55 g almond flour
- 55 g butter, at room temperature
- 2 eggs
- 1 teaspoon vanilla essence
- ¼ teaspoon ground cardamom
- ¼ teaspoon ground cloves
- Cooking spray

Instructions:

1. Preheat the air fryer to 184°C. Coat a baking pan with cooking spray.
2. Combine all the ingredients except the oil in a large bowl and stir until well blended. Spoon the batter mixture into the baking pan.
3. Bake in the preheated air fryer for approximately 13 minutes. Check the tart for doneness: If a toothpick inserted into the center of the tart comes out clean, it's done.
4. Remove from the air fryer and place on a wire rack to cool. Serve immediately.

Peanut Butter, Honey & Banana Toast

Serves 4

Prep time: 10 minutes / Cook time: 9 minutes

Ingredients:
- 2 tablespoons unsalted butter, softened
- 4 slices white bread
- 4 tablespoons peanut butter
- 2 bananas, peeled and thinly sliced
- 4 tablespoons honey
- 1 teaspoon ground cinnamon

Instructions:
1. Spread butter on one side of each slice of bread, then peanut butter on the other side. Arrange the banana slices on top of the peanut butter sides of each slice (about 9 slices per toast). Drizzle honey on top of the banana and sprinkle with cinnamon.
2. Cut each slice in half lengthwise so that it will better fit into the air fryer basket. Arrange two pieces of bread, butter sides down, in the air fryer basket. Set the air fryer to 192°C cooking for 5 minutes. Then set the air fryer to 204°C and cook for an additional 4 minutes, or until the bananas have started to brown. Repeat with remaining slices. Serve hot.

Mixed Berry Hand Pies

Serves 4

Prep time: 5 minutes / Cook time: 30 minutes

Ingredients:
- 150 g granulated sugar
- ½ teaspoon ground cinnamon
- 1 tablespoon cornflour
- 150 g blueberries
- 150 g blackberries
- 150 g raspberries, divided into two equal portions
- 1 teaspoon water
- 1 package refrigerated shortcrust pastry (or your own homemade pastry)
- 1 egg, beaten

Instructions:
1. Combine the sugar, cinnamon, and cornstarch in a small saucepan. Add the blueberries, blackberries, and ½ of the raspberries. Toss the berries gently to coat them evenly. Add the teaspoon of water to the saucepan and turn the stovetop on to medium-high heat, stirring occasionally. Once the berries break down, release their juice, and start to simmer (about 5 minutes), simmer for another couple of minutes and then transfer the mixture to a bowl, stir in the remaining ½ of the raspberries and let it cool.
2. Preheat the air fryer to 188°C.
3. Cut the pie dough into four 5-inch circles and four 6-inch circles.
4. Spread the 6-inch circles on a flat surface. Divide the berry filling between all four circles. Brush the perimeter of the dough circles with a little water. Place the 5-inch circles on top of the filling and press the perimeter of the dough circles together to seal. Roll the edges of the bottom circle up over the top circle to make a crust around the filling. Press a fork around the crust to make decorative indentations and to seal the crust shut. Brush the pies with egg wash and sprinkle a little sugar on top. Poke a small hole in the center of each pie with a paring knife to vent the dough.
5. Air fry two pies at a time. Brush or spray the air fryer basket with oil and place the pies into the basket. Air fry for 9 minutes. Turn the pies over and air fry for another 6 minutes. Serve warm or at room temperature.

Crispy Pineapple Rings

Serves 6

Prep time: 5 minutes / Cook time: 6 to 8 minutes

Ingredients:

- 240 ml rice milk
- 85 g plain flour
- 120 ml water
- 25 g unsweetened flaked coconut
- 4 tablespoons granulated sugar
- ½ teaspoon baking soda
- ½ teaspoon baking powder
- ½ teaspoon vanilla essence
- ½ teaspoon ground cinnamon
- ¼ teaspoon ground star anise
- Pinch of kosher, or coarse sea salt
- 1 medium pineapple, peeled and sliced

Instructions:

1. Preheat the air fryer to 192ºC.
2. In a large bowl, stir together all the ingredients except the pineapple.
3. Dip each pineapple slice into the batter until evenly coated.
4. Arrange the pineapple slices in the basket and air fry for 6 to 8 minutes until golden brown.
5. Remove from the basket to a plate and cool for 5 minutes before serving warm

Lemon Curd Pavlova

Serves 4

Prep time: 10 minutes / Cook time: 1 hour

Ingredients:

- Shell:
- 3 large egg whites
- ¼ teaspoon cream of tartar
- 75 g powdered sweetener
- 1 teaspoon grated lemon zest
- 1 teaspoon lemon extract
- Lemon Curd:
- 100 g powdered sweetener
- 120 ml lemon juice
- 4 large eggs
- 120 ml coconut oil
- For Garnish (Optional):
- Blueberries
- powdered sweetener

Instructions:

1. Preheat the air fryer to 135ºC. Thoroughly grease a pie pan with butter or coconut oil.
2. Make the shell: In a small bowl, use a hand mixer to beat the egg whites and cream of tartar until soft peaks form. With the mixer on low, slowly sprinkle in the sweetener and mix until it's completely incorporated.
3. Add the lemon zest and lemon extract and continue to beat with the hand mixer until stiff peaks form.
4. Spoon the mixture into the greased pie pan, then smooth it across the bottom, up the sides, and onto the rim to form a shell. Bake for 1 hour, then turn off the air fryer and let the shell stand in the air fryer for 20 minutes. (The shell can be made up to 3 days ahead and stored in an airtight container in the refrigerator, if desired.)
5. While the shell bakes, make the lemon curd: In a medium-sized heavy-bottomed saucepan, whisk together the sweetener, lemon juice, and eggs. Add the coconut oil and place the pan on the stovetop over medium heat. Once the oil is melted, whisk constantly until the mixture thickens and thickly coats the back of a spoon, about 10 minutes. Do not allow the mixture to come to a boil.
6. Pour the lemon curd mixture through a fine-mesh strainer into a medium-sized bowl. Place the bowl inside a larger bowl filled

with ice water and whisk occasionally until the curd is completely cool, about 15 minutes.

7. Place the lemon curd on top of the shell and garnish with blueberries and powdered sweetener, if desired. Store leftovers in the refrigerator for up to 4 days.

Honeyed, Roasted Apples with Walnuts

Serves 4

Prep time: 5 minutes / Cook time: 12 to 15 minutes

Ingredients:

- 2 Granny Smith apples
- 20 g certified gluten-free rolled oats
- 2 tablespoons honey
- ½ teaspoon ground cinnamon
- 2 tablespoons chopped walnuts
- Pinch salt
- 1 tablespoon olive oil

Instructions:

1. Preheat the air fryer to 192ºC.
2. Core the apples and slice them in half.
3. In a medium bowl, mix together the oats, honey, cinnamon, walnuts, salt, and olive oil.
4. Scoop a quarter of the oat mixture onto the top of each half apple.
5. Place the apples in the air fryer basket, and roast for 12 to 15 minutes, or until the apples are fork tender.

Grilled Pineapple Dessert

Serves 4

Prep time: 5 minutes / Cook time: 12 minutes

Ingredients:

- Coconut, or avocado oil for misting, or

cooking spray
- 4½-inch-thick slices fresh pineapple, core removed
- 1 tablespoon honey
- ¼ teaspoon brandy, or apple juice
- 2 tablespoons slivered almonds, toasted
- Vanilla frozen yogurt, coconut sorbet, or ice cream

Instructions:

1. Spray both sides of pineapple slices with oil or cooking spray. Place into air fryer basket.
2. Air fry at 200ºC for 6 minutes. Turn slices over and cook for an additional 6 minutes.
3. Mix together the honey and brandy.
4. Remove cooked pineapple slices from air fryer, sprinkle with toasted almonds, and drizzle with honey mixture.
5. Serve with a scoop of frozen yogurt or sorbet on the side.

Apple Hand Pies

Serves 8

Prep time: 15 minutes / Cook time: 25 minutes

Ingredients:

- 2 apples, cored and diced
- 60 ml honey
- 1 teaspoon ground cinnamon
- 1 teaspoon vanilla extract
- ⅛ teaspoon ground nutmeg
- 2 teaspoons cornflour
- 1 teaspoon water
- 1 sheet shortcrust pastry cut into 4
- Cooking oil spray

Instructions:

1. Insert the crisper plate into the basket and the basket into the unit. Preheat the unit to 204ºC.
2. In a metal bowl that fits into the basket,

stir together the apples, honey, cinnamon, vanilla, and nutmeg.

3. In a small bowl, whisk the cornflour and water until the cornflour dissolves.

4. Once the unit is preheated, place the metal bowl with the apples into the basket.

5. cook for 2 minutes then stir the apples. Resume cooking for 2 minutes.

6. Remove the bowl and stir the cornflour mixture into the apples. Reinsert the metal bowl into the basket and resume cooking for about 30 seconds until the sauce thickens slightly.

7. When the cooking is complete, refrigerate the apples while you prepare the piecrust.

8. Cut each piecrust into 2 (4-inch) circles. You should have 8 circles of crust.

9. Lay the piecrusts on a work surface. Divide the apple filling among the piecrusts, mounding the mixture in the center of each round.

10. Fold each piecrust over so the top layer of crust is about an inch short of the bottom layer. (The edges should not meet.) Use the back of a fork to seal the edges.

11. Insert the crisper plate into the basket and the basket into the unit. Preheat the unit 204ºC again.

12. Once the unit is preheated, spray the crisper plate with cooking oil, line the basket with baking paper, and spray it with cooking oil. Working in batches, place the hand pies into the basket in a single layer.

13. Cook the pies for 10 minutes.

14. When the cooking is complete, let the hand pies cool for 5 minutes before removing from the basket.

15. Repeat steps 12, 13, and 14 with the remaining pies.

Double Chocolate Brownies

Serves 8

Prep time: 5 minutes / Cook time: 15 to 20 minutes

Ingredients:

- 110 g almond flour
- 50 g unsweetened cocoa powder
- ½ teaspoon baking powder
- 35 g powdered sweetener
- ¼ teaspoon salt
- 110 g unsalted butter, melted and cooled
- 3 eggs
- 1 teaspoon vanilla extract
- 2 tablespoons mini semisweet chocolate chips

Instructions:

1. Preheat the air fryer to 176ºC. Line a cake pan with baking paper and brush with oil.

2. In a large bowl, combine the almond flour, cocoa powder, baking powder, sweetener, and salt. Add the butter, eggs, and vanilla. Stir until thoroughly combined (the batter will be thick.) Spread the batter into the prepared pan and scatter the chocolate chips on top.

3. Air fry for 15 to 20 minutes until the edges are set (the center should still appear slightly undercooked.) Let cool completely before slicing. To store, cover and refrigerate the brownies for up to 3 days.

Printed in Great Britain
by Amazon

21702231R00052